Please Write

Finding Joy and Meaning in the Soulful Art of Handwritten Letters

Lynne M. Kolze

Disclaimer: Parts of this work depict the actual life of the author. They represent the author's present recollections of experiences over time. Some names and characteristics have been omitted to protect the privacy of the persons discussed, some events have been compressed, and some dialogue has been re-created to the best of the author's abilities.

Edited by Sara Ensey.

ISBN 13: 978-1-64343-673-9
Library of Congress Catalog Number: 2023901695
Printed in the United States of America
First Printing: 2023
27 26 25 24 23 5 4 3 2 1

Book design and typesetting by Dan Pitts.
The Marcel typeface used for chapter headings was created by Carolyn Porter.

Beaver's Pond Press
939 Seventh Street West
Saint Paul, MN 55102
(952) 829-8818
www.BeaversPondPress.com

Contact Lynne M. Kolze at LynneKolze.com for speaking engagements, book club discussions, freelance writing projects, and interviews.

To my parents,
Natalie and Larry,
who showed me how to communicate from the heart.

To Randall Baker (1944–2020),
a faithful correspondent for thirty-five years:
a letter enthusiast, brilliant writer with great wit,
and an astute observer of the world.

Contents

SECTION 1—INTRODUCTION

Introduction 1

Why We Still Need Letters 5

A Treasured Memento 9

A Circle of Gratitude 15

SECTION 2—THE LEGACY OF LETTER WRITING

Skip the Gym: Why Letter Writing Is Good for Us 21

The Joy of Anticipation 25

Letters Are a Learning Laboratory 29

Letter Writing as Spiritual Practice 37

Ink Reveals Our Imperfections 41

Letters Can Save Lives 45

Letters Encourage Our Development 49

Old Letters Reveal Our Core Truths 55

Letters: Our Accidental Memoirs 59

A "Flowery Letter" Never Forgotten 65

SECTION 3—LETTERS WE REMEMBER

A Letter to You by Julie Kolze Sorensen 73

Thank-You Letters:
Why Showing Appreciation Never Goes Out of Style 75

Gratitude Letters: Beyond the Simple Thank-You 79

Letters from Our Grandmothers 87

Be Still My Heart: Long Live the Love Letter 97

A Soldier's Letters Home 107

Letters from a Stranger 113

The Sympathy Letter 119

Letters That Hurt 123

Letters That Heal 131

Pen Pal Letters: A Whole New World Awaits 139

The Round Robin: The Letter That Keeps on Giving 145

The Legacy Letter 149

A Letter to the Future: The Time Capsule Letter 159

SECTION 4—LETTERS INSPIRE ART

Artful Flourishes We Don't Forget 167

Doodles, Drawings, and Other Delights 175

Letters That Think Outside the Envelope 185

Mail Art 189

Epistolary Art 193

SECTION 5—THE CURIOUS, QUIRKY, AND FASCINATING WORLD OF LETTER WRITING

A Short History of the Letter 201

The Postmark/Stamp Cancel 213

The Postcard: A Simple Feast for the Eyes 217

A Letter to the Bridegroom's Oak 223

Sending Letters to a Neighborhood Elf 227
The Subtle, Loving Language of . . . a *Postage Stamp*? 231
The Bird-Brained Letter Carrier 237
W. Reginald Bray: The Human Letter 241
Letters Lost and Found 247
Mailboxes That Spark Delight 251

SECTION 6—WRITING THE NEW AND PRESERVING THE OLD
Encouraging the Next Generation of Letter Writers 259
Letter Writing in a Sea of Distractions 263
Tips for Preserving Old Letters 269
Simply No Substitute 275

Final Words 281

Epilogue 285
Acknowledgments 289
Image Credits 291
Endnotes 293
About the Author 307

Introduction

Introduction

When I told people that I was writing a book about handwritten letters, some of them could not hide their skepticism, probably because handwritten letters seem about as relevant to their lives now as eight-track tapes. Still, and somewhat surprisingly perhaps, many more people had a different reaction—an undeniably positive response. With smiles and delight, these letter enthusiasts happily shared heartfelt experiences related to sending and receiving handwritten letters. They told me deeply personal, sometimes even transformative stories about the impact a certain letter or collection of letters had on their lives. There were stories of changed lives, filled hearts, unforgettable kindnesses, deep passions, even terminated relationships—all because of letters.

With a long exhale and a sense of sadness and resignation, my fellow letter enthusiasts then lamented the end of the "golden age" of handwritten correspondence. Perhaps you, too, have long ago given up on the idea that handwritten letters could be part of your life. If so, I encourage you to look at recent societal trends. There is a glimmer of hope on the horizon; younger generations are showing a renewed enthusiasm for handwritten correspondence, and I, for one, am optimistic about the future of handwritten letters.

During the first year of the COVID-19 pandemic in 2020, for example, sales of cards and stationery thrived, according to recent surveys.[1] "Everyone is experiencing digital fatigue, which is real—so we are turning to tangible things," market analyst Andrea Bell explains. "And we have more time on our hands than ever before. We are experiencing moments of self-reflection and quiet, and for many, using that time to send a card or letter feels like the right thing to do."[2]

To me, letters represent something deeper, more lasting, and more meaningful than other kinds of communication. Specifically, they give voice to our deepest emotions, encourage our creativity and most earnest self-expression, and enable us to share love from the depths of our souls. Letters symbolize connections, intimacy, caring, commitment, and sharing with others, heart to heart and mind to mind. The letters we write represent and record all that it means to be human—the loves, losses, frustrations, achievements, dreams, sorrows, and existential dilemmas we may face. What could be more important than that?

I am not ready to let go of the handwritten letter. It may seem irrational to some to cling to an old form of communication given the ease, speed, and predictability of computers and smartphones. Yet it is precisely because of the sameness and one-dimensionality of technology that I crave the analog, highly tactile, and the deeply personal nature of handwritten communications. Because you have picked up this book, maybe you do, too.

This book is for letter enthusiasts who regularly write letters, for those people who once loved the letter-writing process but have given up on the activity, as well as for those who are interested in writing letters for the first time. Here, I share my love for handwritten letters through my own personal lens, as well as from the perspectives of artists, authors, historians, storytellers, and other letter lovers. This is not a scholarly review. I do not dwell on the history of letter writing (though it does get a quick overview), tease apart the letters of famous authors, or provide prompts for writing the "perfect letter."

Instead, I explore the meaning and value of handwriting letters from my own and others' experiences, as well as from a broader societal standpoint, driven by my curiosity and a desire to celebrate a form of communication that has linked humanity for thousands of years. When used with positive intent, a letter's greatest value is as a platform for the best of who we are at our most authentic, loving, and playful selves.

I encourage anyone who adores letter writing to dust off your old—or pick up a new—favorite pen and add some joy to the lives of the people you know and hold dear. Letters are one of the greatest gifts we can give. Why not initiate a new, positive, and loving exchange with someone you adore—family, lovers, neighbors, friends—using one of the oldest, most authentic forms of interpersonal communication there is?

Dear readers, please, do write!

Why We Still Need Letters

During periods of my life, I have had a fear of abandonment. It is irrational in many ways given that I was raised in a secure, loving family and supported by many caring relatives in my large extended family. I have always had wonderful friends. My own nuclear family has brought me great happiness. Perhaps it is the thought of losing those connections somehow that made me so fearful.

This fear may be something I cannot control. After all, our brains are hardwired for connection and community. From these, we derive a sense of safety and belonging, which human beings have needed to survive and thrive for millennia. We need each other, plain and simple.

Because of the COVID-19 pandemic, many of us can now say that we have a deep, personal experience with loneliness. The pandemic tested our ability to be resilient and kind with one another in the face of a serious health threat. Most of us have found ways to adapt reasonably well and to cope with the situation at hand. Yet many of us could also say with impunity that we never want to be separated from our loved ones for that long or to be that lonely ever again. We now understand how easily darkness can creep into our lives if we become too disconnected from our friends, relatives, coworkers, and community.

Too much alone time, whatever the circumstance—pandemics, illness, disability, relationship breakups, old age, living far from our people—is never good for us long term. In fact, it is often detrimental to our health. Being alone and lonely can increase the risks for depression, cognitive impairment, accelerated aging, and premature death. It causes higher levels of inflammation, hypertension, heart problems, and anxiety.[3] Medical research supports the notion that we need to be connected to each other to be well, that we need each other from our first breaths on this planet to our last good-byes.

Through our social networks and connections or by simply watching the news, it's easy to see that there is a good deal of loneliness and despair in this world. Recent studies have shown that at any given time, as many as three out of five Americans describe themselves as lonely.[4] So it's important to do whatever we can in both small and more significant ways to help soothe some of this pain and actively strive to build better connections with one another.

Over my lifetime, I've listened to countless stories of loneliness, conflict, disconnection, estrangement, and loss from my friends and colleagues. I have often felt great empathy, wishing for ways to offer them support, since this lifelong journey can be too difficult for many of us to travel alone.

Now, you might ask, how does this relate to letter writing?

Love and caring *can* fit into an envelope. Writing personal, handwritten letters is a unique expression of caring. If we fully open our hearts and minds in the process of letter writing, we may find that giving and receiving love gets a little easier all the time. Through our authentic communications, we can be rewarded with more nurturing and fulfilling relationships throughout our lives. Research shows that having satisfying, reliable relationships is the most important indicator of a happy life.[5]

Developing satisfying and deep, personal connections is reason enough for writing handwritten letters, but they offer us much more. There is the visual delight they offer, the writing and storytelling skills they develop, the history they document, and the springboard they create for the arts, among many other things.

Let's reacquaint ourselves with this lovely form of communication. Let's embrace "the old," the "outdated" when it makes sense to do so. It is time to remember what it's like to experience the sweetness, kindness, and intimacy of this highly personal form of communication. We need this now more than ever in our increasingly challenging, perplexing world.

Please join me in exploring all the things that make letter writing one of the most gratifying, generous, and soulful forms of communication ever created. Then let's use this tried-and-true communication tool to show our commitment to taking care of each other and provide needed support and entertainment to those we hold dear.

A Treasured Memento

It seems to me that there is a very great significance in letter-writing, and that it differs from daily intercourse as the dramatic differs from the epic or narrative. It is the life of man, and above all the chief part of his life, his inner life.

—John Stuart Mill

Imagine this scenario: a wildfire is moving your way, burning quickly through the dry brush in the hills around your home. The local authorities have given you two hours to vacate the premises. There is a serious chance you will lose everything you own. You must prioritize what to take with you. You must make some quick decisions.

What is most valuable? What is most irreplaceable? What has intrinsic value beyond dollars and cents?

Many of us would undoubtedly pack things like money, pet supplies, legal papers, photographs, scrapbooks, jewelry, family heirlooms, and other key memorabilia from our lives.

If we had the time, we would probably also grab that box of old letters at the back of the closet—the ones from spouses, parents, former lovers, relatives, good friends. The idea of losing something as irreplaceable and precious as old letters would be devastating. Why? I believe it is because letters are a deeply personal symbol of someone's life. They contain the essence of their authors.

Letters are windows into our souls. They provide the space for people to reveal what is deep inside of them—the place where they can be vulnerable, "naked," their own true selves without the fear of public judgment.

If I lost my old letters, I would be losing a special part of the people I love—the better part of them in many ways. This is the reason my box of old letters would be one of the first things I would grab in case of fire or flood. Losing them would mean losing more than just a box of paper.

People treasure cards and letters for a host of reasons. Short messages jotted on an attractive card can be just as memorable and impactful as a much longer missive. You might have once received a quick note of appreciation for something you did, and those words have stayed with you for a lifetime.

A successful businesswoman friend of mine, for example, once received a thank-you note from her second-grade teacher. "I remember helping her sort through some books and clean bookshelves in the classroom," she shares. "I was happy to help. A few days later, Mrs. Anderson gave me a box with a card attached. Inside the card, she had written: 'Thank you so much for all your help. I so appreciate it. Here's a little gift as a way to thank you for your kindness. Sincerely, Mrs. Anderson.'"

Because my friend had a difficult childhood, any small gesture of thoughtfulness or caring mattered a great deal to her. "It didn't really matter what was in the box," she says. "Nothing could top that note! But of course, I did open the box to find a beautiful, hand-embroidered handkerchief inside. I have kept the letter and the box that held the handkerchief for fifty years. Why? I suppose it was because my family members weren't very kind to each other, and we certainly didn't show appreciation for one another. Mrs. Anderson's message and gift meant the world to me at the time. She made me feel special and important—something I didn't often experience. I am sure my teacher had no idea how much that short note and small gift meant to me. I bet she would be surprised to learn that I have kept it all these years."

Sometimes, a little bit of effort can fill a hungry heart. That teacher's kind gesture lit a way for my friend to find self-love, romantic love, and acceptance outside her nuclear family.

I've often asked myself why it has been so difficult for me to let go of my attachment to handwritten letters. I have handwritten hundreds of letters over my lifetime and typed thousands more documents on a computer. Logically, the computer wins hands down in terms of ease, practicality, and speed. Handwritten letters, on the other hand, typically take more focused attention and require me to first locate paper, pen, and a stamp before I begin, then require some physical effort on my part to mail. So why do I keep writing my letters by hand?

Heart.

Letters represent love. Tidy, computer-generated letters leave me cold. They lack heart—the warmth, personality, charm, and playfulness of the paper letter. I have never found them to be quite as emotionally satisfying to write or receive.

Letters remain special treasures because they are rare, deeply personal, one-of-a-kind creations that cannot be replaced if lost or destroyed. Most of us do not feel the same attachment to a typewritten or emailed letter. People seem to most value things made by hand, knowing that someone had to go to a greater level of effort and spend more of their valuable time creating something just for them. In these overscheduled times, we naturally appreciate that extra effort.

The generations of people who used letter writing as their main form of communication are mostly gone now or, for the most part, have made the switch to electronic forms of communication. These folks have changed with the times, as we would expect them to. However, when I ask those same people how they feel about the art of handwritten letters, many become nostalgic. They have an inner knowing that we've lost something important when we converted from pen, ink, and stationery to computer screens.

Some might assume that those who still cling to pen and paper are just an obstinate bunch who have trouble making a shift. I believe our stubbornness is more than a simple aversion to change. People who are well acquainted with handwritten letters understand that letters are uniquely expressive offerings unlike any other. Many of them still happily write that occasional letter, and I've found new hope in the fact that younger generations are returning to some old-school activities like typewritten and, yes, even handwritten cards and letters.

Even more surprising are the young men who show an interest in letters. On a recent summer day, two young, tough-looking moving men came to our house to remove a hideously heavy piece of unwanted furniture from our living room. One of them was particularly chatty and worked at making polite conversation with me as we closed the deal. He asked how I planned to spend the rest of my day. I mentioned writing this book, but I must be honest: I hesitated for a moment before telling him what the book was about, because I imagined him and his partner huddled out of sight by their truck, doubled over in laughter.

But I threw caution to the wind. "I'm writing a book about handwritten letters," I said, expecting blank stares.

Quite surprisingly, the more talkative mover responded with a large, genuine smile. "Really? That's cool! I just love getting real letters. I would read a book like that." The other mover smiled and agreed. "I'll try to look it up sometime!" he said.

I could have been pushed over with a feather.

I had stereotyped these young gentlemen as having zero interest in letter writing. But their reaction speaks to the universal desire for real, intimate forms of communication and connection.

On another day, an acupuncture specialist related that her son, a recent college graduate, regularly penned letters to several women he had known in college. In fact, these women had given him an ultimatum: "Either write us letters, or we just won't communicate!" This story was music to my ears.

Other Hopeful Signs for Letter Lovers

In recent years, the Bond Handwritten Note Service surveyed two thousand adults about their practices and feelings regarding handwritten correspondence. Among their findings:[6]

- About one-third of adults have not received a handwritten note in more than a year.
- Fifteen percent have not written a note or letter in more than five years.

However, interestingly, the survey also found:

- Eighty-one percent of respondents feel that handwritten notes are more meaningful than email, texts, and the like.
- Eighty-seven percent of millennials value handwritten correspondence above all other ways of communicating.

These facts seem utterly counterintuitive given our predilection for fast and furious communications in a high-tech world. But it turns out that millennials are part of a small but seemingly growing movement of people who would like to return to a more tangible, affirming method of communication. Interestingly, millennials are more likely than people in their fifties to hang on to handwritten notes and letters.[7] It is no wonder. Letters, for their generation, are rare and precious commodities indeed.

Letters and Computers: A Peaceful Coexistence?

Over the years, I have been delighted by people of all ages who have shared their stories about the letters they have received—letters that created intimacy and connection or sparked romantic love with someone dear to them. Nearly everyone said that they have carefully stored these letters (especially love letters) in attics, file cabinets, and closets in homes, apartments, and retirement communities across America.

As I've mentioned, a subset of the population has stubbornly clung to letter writing—but not at the expense of technology's conveniences. I, for one, happily use both. There is no earthly reason why a box of beautiful stationery, ink pens, and stamps cannot be at the ready on our computer desks. When we most value speed and efficiency, we can reach for our smartphones and computers. However, if our goal is to create or deepen our relationships and our most valued connections with others, let's instead make an intentional effort to take the time to write that special letter or card.

We *can* reclaim letter writing again, fitting it into our lives when we are inspired.

We *can* choose to give those we love the irreplaceable gift that a letter is and, in the process, feel how wonderful it is to give our time and attention to someone else, to focus deeply on that person as we write, and to feel a deep gratitude for their impact on our lives.

A Circle of Gratitude

It was Christmastime, and I was searching for a new cookie recipe because a close friend was coming the next day for a cooperative holiday baking extravaganza. I opened my cabinet and found an older cookbook, one I had seldom, if ever, used before. I hoped it might hold an amazing recipe that my friend might also enjoy. I cracked open the shiny, flawless binding and noticed something inside the front cover. There, in my mother's perfect handwriting, was an inscription to my daughter and me, long forgotten:

To Lynne and Laura—Our two wonderful cooks
With love, Grandma and Grandpa Kolze, Christmas, 2009.

Her inscription was short, but it spoke volumes about the caring person my mother was. She always paid great attention to the intangibles, the micro-gestures that make up a loving life. I smiled, thinking about the ways her artful handwriting reflected her intense love of beauty and home, the importance she placed on a gracious but unpretentious style of living, and her impeccable manners, which made her an enjoyable companion and friend to all.

In that moment, I felt joyful and sad at the same time. I lingered there on the cover page, happy to see this two-dimensional reminder of her and wishing I could share a cup of afternoon tea with her just once more. Moving my fingers over her written words was as close as I could come to holding her hand again, the same way I had during the last weeks of her life as she slowly slipped away from us.

Everything I know about writing letters and thank-you cards and domesticity I learned from my mother's tutelage and example. All the lessons she taught me, which were often devalued by society during the 1960s and 1970s, have been the cornerstones of my own contented life. She taught me that beauty in our surroundings and in our deeds create a rewarding life. What my mother focused on was creating a heart-centered space built on caring, compassion, and growth.

My mother's focus on the home, her family, and the guests who visited us rippled out in many directions. Through her example, I have worked hard to create a home as welcoming to friends and family as hers was. So, it is no wonder that I have come to savor the small moments of joy, like baking cookies in my kitchen with a wonderful friend.

The morning after I found the special cookbook, my friend arrived, loaded down with a box of goodies to bake with, recipes, cookie sheets, and a can-do spirit. Balancing on top of it all was a medium-size corrugated box from a big-box store. "I brought you something—to get your creative juices flowing for your book project," she said. "It's a box of my old letters I wanted to show you."

"I can't wait to see them," I remarked. She, like me, has written hundreds of letters over the years and saved all the letters she received over her lifetime.

We dutifully and rather absentmindedly made our cookie dough, lining up the cookie sheets in succession, getting them ready for baking as we talked. Once several batches had finished baking, we settled down to our cups of tea. She opened her treasured box of letters. Inside the box was layer upon layer of different-colored envelopes, some bejeweled with colorful stamps and lovely cursive writing.

In an incredibly generous show of trust and openness, my friend offered to read me some of her letters. She selected an interesting variety of letters—everything from her letters at camp, chatty letters from her mother, loving cards from her father, college friends, boyfriends, a pastor, and an aunt. Letters simply document people's stories, and I have always been fascinated with stories, all stories. So, this was as much a treat for me as it was for her.

As my friend read me these letters from long ago, I watched the expressions on her face. In the middle of reading, she would suddenly smile, reveling in a special memory or in the author's great humor. Other times, she was wistful. I was impressed by how eloquent and warm these letters were and how well the writers expressed their feelings and crafted their anecdotes, no matter their background, age, or level of education. My friend's letters also told me a great deal about the depth of her personality and how much others appreciated the same qualities I did. My understanding of her wonderful and unique spirit only expanded thanks to these letters she shared on that delightful day.

A week after our baking extravaganza and letter-sharing event was over, my friend, her husband, my husband, and I were all gathered around the Christmas tree, watching the crackling fire and engaging in a freewheeling conversation that touched on a diverse set of topics. Before our visit was over, my friend reached into her purse and pulled out a surprise gift for me. Inside the wrapping paper, there was a set of beautiful envelopes, each made from attractive paper ephemera she found at home. This was the perfect gift to complete a wonderful holiday week.

Later, as I placed my friend's pretty, handcrafted envelopes into my desk's cubbyhole, I thought about how much my mother would have loved the creative and thoughtful nature of her handmade gift. In fact, as I write this chapter, I hear my mother's voice in my ear, saying, "Now, don't forget to write a nice thank-you card to your friend for making you those lovely envelopes. Her thoughtfulness and generosity should be acknowledged."

And so, I did.

The Legacy of Letter Writing

Skip the Gym:
Why Letter Writing Is Good for Us

We all have days when we cannot muster the energy or the enthusiasm to go to the gym or go outside in the snow and cold to take our daily walk. Inertia can be a hard thing to overcome. Should you feel guilty? Should you be concerned that your health will suffer because of your procrastination? Or that your lethargy and idle habits will increase the stress you already feel?

I say no!

When enthusiasm for physical exercise, sweating, and pain temporarily wanes, feel no shame. Instead, do yourself and someone else a favor. Write a letter.

"What?" you say. "How in the world could sitting at a desk, lifting, and pushing a one-ounce pen and slowly scribbling on paper possibly be good for me?" To tell the truth, letter writing will never be as good for you as movement and aerobic exercise, but in a pinch, letter writing (a.k.a. communicating) does have its health benefits.

Consider writing a letter as a pleasant, meditative way to ease your stress. Using ink and writing on paper requires quietude, focus,

and attention. Handwriting can help to calm your mind, sharpen your writing skills, and make sense of memories and feelings at the same time. Writing can create order out of internal chaos and calm the internal chatter that creates the stress in the first place. Writing letters can be just as soothing, calming, and meditative as knitting, drawing, or painting.

Writing a letter using pen and paper can also be restful for your overworked eyes. Research has shown that our eyes suffer from the endless hours we spend staring at screens. Children are becoming increasingly near-sighted because the hours spent looking at computers begin so much earlier in their formative lives, and exposure lasts for longer and longer periods of time as they get older.[8]

In addition, research suggests that people who still write letters by hand are happier than people who do not. Does this surprise us? I think not. Letters often contain expressive words of love, caring, rousing good humor, sadness, gratitude—words that bear witness to the complexity of being human. With letters, we give something of ourselves, contribute to something bigger than ourselves.

According to Kent State professor Steven Toepfer, handwriting letters that express gratitude and thank-you notes to people we value helps to decrease feelings of depression and anxiety. In fact, he says, expressive writing often leads to fewer health problems, improved immune system responses to illness, higher levels of life satisfaction, and even better grades.[9]

Toepfer ran an experiment with six groups of students, having each of them write a letter of gratitude to someone who had made a difference in their lives. Each student had to write a letter every two weeks for six weeks. The letters had to be expressive, positive, and thoughtful while conveying a sense of gratitude and appreciation for the person they were writing to. After each batch of letters was mailed, Toepfer surveyed his students on how the experience affected their moods, sense of well-being, and gratitude. With each additional letter, he said, students' levels of happiness increased.[10]

"The more they wrote, the better they felt," Toepfer says. "The most powerful thing in our lives is our social network. It doesn't have to be large, and you don't always need to be the life of the party, but just having one or two significant connections in your life has shown to have terrific psychological and physical benefits."[11]

Letters are good for us and the people we admire and love. Could there be a bigger win-win? So, get to the gym sometimes, but know that both exercise and letter writing are good for you—body *and* soul.

The Joy of Anticipation

We want things. And we want them now—yesterday, if possible. After all, why would we want to postpone gratification or wait to meet a need if we don't have to? When a person's well-being is at stake, there is clearly no benefit to waiting for something that will ease suffering.

However, most things we want in life could wait a day or two or longer, and the waiting might just make the recipient feel something oddly exciting, called *anticipation*.

Research shows that looking forward to something makes people happy and helps us to lead more positive lives. Psychology researchers Van Boven and Ashworth found that people are more likely to have intense, positive emotions *before* an event happens rather than after the fact. That is because most of us expect that future events will make us happier than those we've experienced in our past. Van Boven and Ashworth believe that anticipation can give people a greater sense of well-being and increase satisfaction with their lives.[12] I have always believed this to be so.

The feelings of delightful anticipation were part of my early experiences. My brother and I spent countless hours carefully reviewing the toy section of the Sears and Ward's Christmas catalogs so we could make our annual lists for Santa Claus. As the days inched closer to Christmas, my anticipation increased, leading to the delight of finding one or two of the toys I had asked for under the Christmas tree.

Around the time of my birthday each year, I happily anticipated the arrival of birthday cards in the mail from my grandparents, who lived far enough away that visiting us for every birthday was not practical or convenient. There was a sense of excitement, appreciation, and joy as I tore open their simple birthday greetings.

In junior high and high school, I waited with great anticipation for the beautiful letters from my pen pal, Brigitte, in France. It was always a thrill to see the colorful aerograms arrive in our mailbox.

During my first year at the University of Wisconsin, I lived in a dorm for juniors and seniors. I was a long way from home and could not return as often as I would have liked. That year, letters were a lifeline that kept me feeling connected to my "people." Each day, after classes were over, I walked back to the dorm, entered the lobby, and made a quick beeline for the bank of mailboxes behind the lobby's main desk. Student mailboxes could only be accessed from a hallway behind the lobby wall. The hallway was quite dark, but the light coming from behind the mailbox cubbies shone through the half-glass mailbox doors, illuminating the contents inside.

As I passed by those mailboxes each day on the way to and from my dorm room, I hoped with all my heart that I would see at least one letter sitting in my box waiting for me. If the space inside my mailbox was filled by a letter or two, my spirits improved considerably, obliterating any feelings of loneliness. If it was empty, I was let down, quite disappointed. I was fortunate that many of my family members and friends were wonderful letter writers, so an empty mailbox did not usually stay that way for long.

But connection also meant that I had to be willing to invest the time on my end, too. So I often made letter writing a priority over my studies. What better way to procrastinate on the physics and calculus homework that gave me such a sense of dread? Rather than

My younger self writing to a college friend, while also enjoying nature—another lifelong passion.

balancing chemistry equations, I was more likely to be hunched over a small pool of light cast downward over my dorm room desk or hidden in the corner of the library stacks, writing letters to friends at far-flung universities.

After graduate school was over, when my husband and I were still dating, we were separated for long periods as we tried to secure our first professional jobs. We were broke most of the time, like students often are. We could not afford the expensive long-distance calls we wanted to make. Instead, we depended on the ever-so-inexpensive letter to stay connected. And at least once or twice a week, a letter from him would wind its way to my mailbox and one or two from me would land in his.

My husband was a dependable and consistent pen pal, filling my mailbox with funny commentary, romantic musings, and dreams of our future together. Each day we were apart, I anxiously approached the mailbox, hoping that one of these treasures awaited me. It was the kind of thrill I have never experienced when receiving a text or email message.

Sometimes our letters would cross in the mail, causing misunderstandings and, at times, a degree of unnecessary pain. Nevertheless, the letters were always worth the wait. The wait and the anticipation only intensified our love and longing until the time when we could be together again.

Many people today would find it unimaginable to wait a week to communicate with someone across the country. Yet, oddly enough, I still get pleasure thinking about those wait times and the circle of caring I felt part of, knowing that the senders cared for me as much as I did them.

You don't need to be George Sand or F. Scott Fitzgerald or particularly eloquent to provide a bit of joy for someone as they gather up the daily mail. What a thrill you will give them! Rather than send yet another corrugated box of predictable, impersonal gifts to those you admire, consider sending an old, time-tested gift instead—a handwritten letter. Better yet, if you can find that special person willing to exchange letters on a regular basis, write on!

By writing letters to someone on a reasonably regular basis, you will be gifting them with that intangible thrill that comes from anticipating the next great letter. Sometimes, *slow is beautiful, the waiting, sublime.*

Letters Are a Learning Laboratory

People who love to read books often enjoy the challenge of writing stories themselves. They might spend a lifetime analyzing the ways gifted authors manage to weave their words into something fantastical or emotionally intense. Reading books written by talented people is a wonderful place to learn about the writing craft.

Mastering the craft, however, comes down to practice, repetitive practice.

Enter the handwritten letter!

By embracing this proven form of communication, we can develop or hone many skills all at once. Handwriting letters improves cursive writing skills (known to increase student achievement), stimulates multiple parts of the brain at once, aids in improving spelling, storytelling, paragraph structure, and expressiveness—not to mention providing a safe place to unload complex or troubled feelings. Ask teachers, relatives, or friends to provide input—the role models who influenced my enjoyment of letter writing certainly helped me!

Earlier generations were letter writers out of necessity. If you wanted contact with relatives or friends across the ocean or even on the other side of the county, you had to send a handwritten letter. Oftentimes, even those who completed only an eighth-grade education had the basic skills needed to craft an eloquent or sweet letter for those back home.

For example, my husband's great-grandmother Laura shared a totally relatable story that can still be appreciated by any new mother or father 130 years later. To her parents and siblings, she wrote:

> *Dear Ones, All at Home,*
>
> *I have just hushed baby Emily off to sleep, but it is very doubtful how many minutes she will sleep! I cannot say baby is any better than she was last week—she is very, very restless. It almost drives me crazy sometimes!*
>
> *Last night, Walter had planned to take us out for a drive and wanted me to be all ready by half-past six. Wait until I give the picture of how ready I was! Face was unwashed, hair rough, dinner dishes partly washed, dining room and kitchen very untidy indeed!*

I have always been of the opinion that we are all born storytellers, like Laura. Letters of early settlers of the United States—soldiers, laborers, teachers, and nurses, for example—are often quite eloquent, emotional, and descriptive.

We will never return to the days when handwritten letters were the primary mode of communicating with one another; however, neither do we need to completely relinquish this handwritten wonder. Technology and the handwritten word can coexist in happy and productive ways.

Letter Writing as a School for Budding Authors

It is no accident that many famous authors (and other artists) are known for their engaging and colorful letters. Their letters were simply another platform to express their innate talents and hone their craft. A small sample of famous authors who are known for their brilliant letters include:

- Frederick Douglass
- Kurt Vonnegut
- Helen Keller
- George Orwell
- Ralph Ellison
- Abraham Lincoln
- Anne Sexton
- Emily Dickinson
- Sylvia Plath
- F. Scott Fitzgerald
- Thomas Jefferson

Consider the last name on this list: Thomas Jefferson, one of the better known of our Founding Fathers. Over his lifetime, he wrote approximately nineteen thousand letters. This is remarkable by any measure. It would be difficult not to improve your writing if you practiced *so* regularly.

One of Jefferson's greatest achievements, of course, was writing the Declaration of Independence. In 1776, members of the Continental Congress appointed him to its Committee of Five. As a member, he was tasked with writing a document that would explain to British king George III why the American colonies wanted to become independent states and separate from the British Empire. The committee consisted of John Adams, Benjamin Franklin, Thomas Jefferson, Robert R. Livingston, and Roger Sherman. Jefferson was chosen to write the declaration because of his "reputation for literature, science, and happy talent for composition." His contemporaries had already noticed that he had a "peculiar felicity of expression." Over seventeen days, Jefferson wrote forty-seven iterations of the declaration, with help from his Committee of Five.

Thomas Jefferson used this desk to write many iterations of the Declaration of Independence in 1776.

None of us will come remotely close to writing nineteen thousand letters in our lifetimes. However, any letters you do write will do wonders to improve your ability to amuse your friends with anecdotes from your vacation from hell and then later, effortlessly respond within the accepted conventions of more formal business correspondence when you need to.

Perhaps you can find someone willing to be a long-term pen pal, like John Adams and Thomas Jefferson. Exchanging letters between pen pals is like cowriting a book that never ends. Each letter you write provides endless opportunities to develop your ideas, your writing style, and to learn how to entertain others with your wit. Your letters also provide the writing prompts so that your pen pal can do the same.

Take it from famous authors: letters are a wonderful way to kill two birds with one stone. You will be able to add joy to someone's day at the same time you are polishing your writing craft.

Penmanship/Cursive Encourages Our Own Unique Style

"My parents each sent letters to me, and they are sentimental items," a respondent from my informal letters survey explains. "My mother attended school in Saskatchewan and Manitoba, Canada, where she said penmanship was valued. She won a handwriting competition, so her letters are beautiful memories."

There is no doubt that our collective skills in penmanship have deteriorated in recent times. Sadly, and I believe wrongly, some elementary schools have stopped teaching cursive writing, believing that children need only typing skills in a technological age. However, current research supports the notion that learning and practicing cursive results in many cognitive benefits that outweigh simple expediency.

Author Dennis Depcik also supports this idea. Of his wife's beautiful handwriting, he observes:

> For me, there was no one who made the same gentle loops of Maggie's L's or the soft curves of her S's. I am sure a computer genius could develop a program that could print in a cursive style that would duplicate Maggie's handwriting, but it wouldn't be the same. It wouldn't be the same because what came from the printer came from a machine, and it could have been printed by anyone. The letters I have from Maggie came from her heart, through her pen to the paper on which they're written. And when I am holding one of Maggie's letters, I'm holding Maggie.[13]

It's true that some people are reluctant to write letters by hand because they are embarrassed by their handwriting. Perhaps they never learned cursive writing in school, or if they did, they are disappointed in themselves for letting their penmanship skills atrophy.

There is no need to worry, my friends. The truth is, no matter what your handwriting looks like (scrawl, chicken scratch), it is ultimately your artistic expression. This is not the 1800s. The headmaster will no longer slap your knuckles with a ruler if your cursive is imperfect!

Thankfully, in our times, handwriting no longer needs to conform to once-rigid rules of penmanship. People will adjust to your unique cursive in the same way they learn to recognize the way you walk, talk, laugh, and gesture. It is part of the package that is uniquely you.

My sister's friend expressed gratitude for her father's handwritten letters. "He had a unique writing style he developed while taking architecture classes," she says. "This distinctive style served him well as his blindness took over in his later years." Something as simple as seeing his unique signature brings back memories of his great warmth and creativity.

It Just Takes Practice!

Writing letters allows us to practice many important skills all at once. But more importantly, our letters become a distinctive personal artifact no one else will ever produce in quite the same way. A piece of mail with a recognizable cursive address relates to a face and a personality the minute we receive it. Later, when we pick up that old letter and read what's inside, we will forever connect it with the special author who created it.

That author could be you.

Isn't it time to dust off your old pen and strengthen your writing skills at the same time?

An Imperfect Letter Is Still Perfect to the Recipient

My letters are far from perfect. Many times, in my younger years, after I had already written several pages of a letter, I suddenly would notice that something had gone completely haywire. The lead sentence of my paragraph started off with good intentions, but suddenly, in a flash, the words went rogue. I had completely veered off topic. I found myself trying to figure out how to get back on topic without making a total fool of myself. Unhappy, I tore several completed pages off the pad, crumpled them up in a huff, and started all over again.

Today, this seems ridiculous to me and explains, perhaps, why letters have the reputation for taking a long time to write. But it was my search for perfection that was the problem. Yes, there are times when we need to pay attention to the beasts of convention—formality, grammar, syntax, for example—when writing formal letters. However, for less formal correspondence, I am now much easier on myself. It is purely human to make mistakes or ramble on now and then on paper, just as I do when I speak. Whatever foibles and quirks we embody in life are welcomed in our letters because they better represent our real selves.

Let's just let it be.

Try to see your personal letter writing as a kind of classroom where you can be free to unwind, make mistakes, and let ideas flow without fear. The nicest thing about writing letters as a means of practicing your writing craft is that you have no formal critic reading your work. The person on the receiving end is likely to be the most forgiving reader of all—and they won't use a red pen to correct you. On the contrary, the person you have written to will likely be thrilled to receive any letter at all.

My fellow writers, let's keep those fingers nimble, our pens filled with ink, and be at the ready to write those letters for special occasions . . . or when the mood strikes us. What better way to build your skill set and dazzle your loved ones at the same time.

Letter Writing as Spiritual Practice

Quiet—boisterous.
Placid—chaotic.
Peaceful—unsettled.
Joyful—grieving.

When I sit down to write letters, I can be in vastly different states of mind. By the time I have finished writing one, I almost invariably feel more grounded and connected, even if things are chaotic or loved ones are far away.

Letter writing has always been a saving grace for me. Putting pen to paper has helped me to find more clarity, self-love, love for others, healing around losses and deaths, gratitude for the things that are working well, and a greater peace of mind in general. When I express my feelings on paper instead of vocalizing them, there is a meditative, spiritual quality to the process—something I do not really have complete control over.

We have all experienced the ways in which the grind of daily life—commuting, working, taking care of others, paying the bills—

can extract psychic energy and diminish our ability to be creative. Sometimes, we don't have the energy left to read a book, much less have time to create new things or contemplate our purpose here.

Yet if I can manage to find the time to sit in a quiet corner and write a letter to someone I care about, I create the space where I will slow down, quiet my mind, and take back some of my sanity in the process. Call it a meditation if you will, because when I write, I find greater calm, focus, and purpose. I have put my complete attention and concentration on just one thing, one person I want to connect with. For a short window of time, they will get all of me.

In contrast, if I decide to call someone on the phone instead, I will catch myself multitasking—loading the dishwasher, getting the mail, wiping the countertops. In these moments, I am not truly present with the person on the phone. Perhaps this is why sending a letter is a profoundly meaningful gift in these distracted times. You simply cannot write a letter and fold the laundry at the same time. For a short time, letter writing requires all your effort, all your focus, solely for the purpose of making someone happy.

There Is Meaning in Ritual

One afternoon during my teen years, as I was helping my grandmother in the kitchen, she told me that washing the dishes was something she did not mind doing at all. I looked at her quizzically. "Yes," she said, "it is a monotonous task, but there is something spiritual about doing menial work. It gives me time to slow down and think, and feel grateful for the food I ate and the home I live in."

At the time, I did not really understand her point. However, now that I am older, I can better understand why she felt that way. Like a sink full of dishes, writing letters also gives you space to be silent, to think your own thoughts, and to focus in that moment on someone other than yourself. Writing letters gives us immediate purpose in life, right here in the present moment. In my view, it is in these moments that letter writing supports a higher spiritual practice and connection with something meaningful outside of ourselves.

Dr. Rachel Naomi Remen, in her beautiful book *Kitchen Table Wisdom*, reminds us, "All of life can become ritual. When it does, our experience of life changes radically and the ordinary becomes consecrated. Ritual doesn't make mystery happen. It helps us see and experience something which is already real. It does not create the sacred, it only describes what is there and always has been there, deeply hidden in the obvious."[14]

In his book, *The Power of Ritual*, author Casper ter Kuile makes a similar point about the importance of simple, repetitive tasks: "I have come to believe that just about anything can become a spiritual practice—gardening, painting, singing, snuggling, sitting. The world is full of these rituals! . . . We just need to be clear about our intention (what are we inviting into this moment?), bring it to our attention (coming back to being present in the moment), and make space for repetition (coming back to this practice time and again). In this way, rituals make the invisible connections that make life meaningful, visible."[15]

Letter writing embodies what is beautiful and sacred about small rituals. While at first the letter writer may seek only to communicate some news with a loved one, with repetition, the writing and exchange of letters will become a meaningful ritual that brings delight to both sender and receiver.

The magic of ritual does not end there, my friends. Once your letter has arrived at its destination, we imagine that certain rituals will take place within the home of the lucky recipient. The layer of junk mail that initially hid your attractive, colorful envelope from view is immediately recycled. Bills are happily forgotten at the moment and shoved aside. A teakettle is set on the stove. Work clothes are traded for an old, soft robe. Plush slippers follow. The addressee sits down with a cup of their favorite tea, ready to enjoy your latest offering.

First, your recipient spends a moment appreciating your attractive envelope and stamps. Your interesting cursive is noted. They run a letter opener under the flap and carefully slice open the envelope. Once your letter is unfolded, the magic happens. They take delight in the playful prose and your news of the day. Once your letter has been read, it might be reread many more times. Next, your letter is put away for safekeeping. And so the ritual ends, the same it always has for time immemorial. Your role in creating this quiet interlude will be forever cherished and surely never forgotten.

Ink Reveals Our Imperfections

Open the drawer of any antique desk, occasional table, or secretary, and you will invariably find evidence of a writer's life. The telltale signs are all there: streaks of black ink dribbled from a malfunctioning fountain pen, a splotch of ink spilled from an overturned bottle. These marks are now and forever a part of the furniture, documenting an important part of human history.

Inks are permanent and unforgiving—and that, I would argue, is mostly a good thing. Had they not been, we would have lost a good deal of our history. But let's be honest, inks are also responsible for creating their share of destruction, cursing, and tears. How many garments, area rugs, furnishings, tablecloths, and more have been ruined by this unruly substance? A careless flick of the finger or overly demonstrative hand gesture sends ink onto the most unwelcomed of surfaces.

Despite its downsides, ink has been a great gift to humanity. It has propelled civilizations to grow and prosper. It has recorded our greatest blunders and our most impressive triumphs. Most

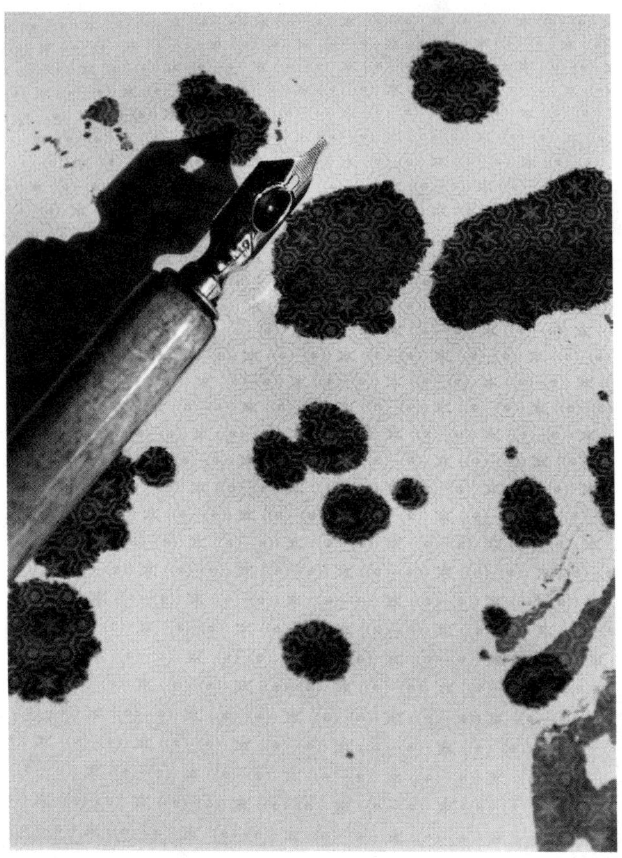

importantly perhaps, it allowed millions of armchair historians to record history through their own personal lenses, and enabled countless more to convey what was deep in their hearts.

The beauty of ink is that it records the best of us as well as our imperfections. Our misspellings, poor word choices, or inappropriate turns of phrase are there for future generations to see and judge. Our anger, passions, joys, and confusions are laid bare on the paper, revealing both our loving and shadow sides.

Ink also reveals the messy edits, the additions and subtractions that are inevitable when we craft handwritten works. These reveal much more about the inner workings of the author's mind than a perfectly spell-checked, typed manuscript ever could.

My father, for example, was an intelligent and expressive man. His ideas, humor, and writing style were quite engaging, but the spelling and grammar were not always so perfect. I now find his letters and writings more interesting and endearing because they include the errors and misspellings. Had he written his letters with a pencil or computer, he could have simply corrected any errors with the flick of his finger. But I would have missed something important about his personality, gifts, and complexities. Imperfect people are more relatable and more realistic. It is their complexity that makes them captivating and compelling figures.

Tidying Up?

Computers now tidy up our imperfections in their cold, terribly efficient way. We have come to depend on machines to give others the illusion that we are perfect people, but we have also sanitized our communications in the process. If we want the art of letter writing to survive, we must fall in love again with the beauty and imperfections of the handwritten word.

Letters Can Save Lives

Is it possible that something as simple as sending handwritten letters to people with suicidal thoughts might keep them from taking their own lives? A small research study conducted on a group of 3,005 psychiatric patients hospitalized between 1969 and 1974 did indeed show such a positive and promising outcome among the survivors of attempted suicides.

This study, which later became known as the Caring Letters Approach, was designed by psychiatrist Jerome Motto and statistician Alan Bostrom, who designed a randomized, controlled experiment among people at high risk of suicide who had refused ongoing treatment.[16] Often, these were people who had already attempted suicide and been hospitalized for treatment.

As the patients were released from the hospital, Motto assigned each person to one of two groups. The patients in Group A, the contact group, each received periodic, personalized handwritten letters from their health care professionals. The letters expressed concern for their well-being and a desire to remain connected through letter writing or telephoning. The letter asked nothing else from the patients. Each patient received eight letters during the first year. In subsequent years, they received four letters a year, for a total of twenty-four letters over five years.

Patients in Group B, the control group, received no letters from health care professionals at all.

In Group B, sadly, 3.52 percent of the patients did go on to kill themselves after release. However, among the group that periodically received the friendly and caring letters, 1.8 percent died by suicide. This may not seem significant; however, given the large size of the patient groups, this meant that nearly twice the number of patients (twenty-nine people) died by suicide in the group that had not received letters compared to the patients (fifteen people) who did.[17]

The effects of showing caring concern in the letters seem to have had an effect that went well beyond two years as well. Interestingly, even when the doctor studied the group up to thirteen years after their initial release from the hospital, patients who had received letters still had lower rates of suicide than those who did not receive letters.[18]

Motto concluded that experiencing caring concern made the contact group feel more connected and accountable to others. That was enough to prevent suicide among twice as many people when comparing the groups.

Apparently, 25 percent of those who received letters shared messages of gratitude with the doctor who sent them. Some patients commented that the letters showed that someone still cared about them and was concerned for their welfare even when it seemed no one else did. The Caring Letters Approach is inexpensive as a preventive approach to suicide and is still only one of a few approaches that scientific research proved is successful during the first two years after someone first attempts to take their life.

Some years later, researcher Kate A. Comtois and her colleagues tried to apply Motto's Caring Letters Approach within a military setting, texting caring messages to 658 active soldiers and marines at risk of suicide. With these patients, each received eleven caring contacts in addition to standard treatments over twelve months. While caring contacts did not show an ability to reduce suicides during the initial twelve-month period, they did end up reducing suicidal ideation by 44 percent during the follow-up period, and there was a 48 percent decrease in suicide attempts compared to those receiving standard care alone.[19]

I am not a doctor. I am also not an expert on suicide prevention. But I was deeply moved when I read about these studies. The idea is simple enough: a letter might save a life. A letter or caring message can make the difference between someone ending their life or, in some cases, deciding to live. For some, this small show of affection and concern is enough to encourage that next step forward.

And even one life saved is worth the effort.

These studies underscore how powerful and important it is to reach out to one another, to let people know that they matter, and they are enough just the way they are. Letters (and in the latter case, texts) are mechanisms to show that we care. The smallest acts of love and caring add up. They are like the silk strings of a web. No one line of thread makes the web strong, but many lines of silk create strength and support for these souls so much in need. The truth is, sometimes we all have these same needs.

If you know someone who is struggling, please consider reaching out to them with the highly personal, potential lifesaver that a letter can be. Your friend, neighbor, or loved one may never forget your efforts.

Letters Encourage Our Development

In recent years, there has been a resurgence of interest in Fred Rogers, the host of the PBS program *Mr. Rogers' Neighborhood.* Several documentaries and Hollywood movies now extol him for his many virtues and fine character. Twenty years ago, I could never have imagined that this would happen, since for most of his life, this man was the butt of jokes and ridicule in the media and pop culture.

I am ashamed to admit that for many years of my youth and early adulthood, I was one of the people who made fun of Fred Rogers. Like many of us, I saw him as an odd duck, a joke. He seemed to be the very personification of a Goody Two-shoes, giving his sensitive, sugary messages during a time in the late 1960s to early 1970s when the entire world seemed to be unraveling from war, civil unrest, and political corruption.

The years passed. Fred Rogers continued to relentlessly pursue his calling, and I followed mine. I never gave him a thought for the next two decades. Then one day, everything changed. I became a mother. During my daughter's toddler and prekindergarten years, she wanted to watch *Mr. Rogers' Neighborhood* in the afternoons when we were home together. Sometimes, I would sit down on the couch with her, folding clothes or attending to other work. I half listened, half cared. However, over time, his songs and sweet voice began to seep into my heart, and I began to see what he had been trying to do for children for all those years.

Fred Rogers's show was quiet, deliberate, and comforting, enveloping you like a warm embrace. His messages were consistently loving, his encouragement purposeful, and his presence always calming. I could easily see how much this grandfatherly figure could mean to children growing up in a chaotic home or with emotionally absent parents—or, frankly, in just about any circumstance, good or bad.

I began to watch the show more analytically than I had in my youth. I finally began to understand that because of his authenticity and caring personality, he created a deep sense of trust with his television audience. He modeled polite and decent behaviors, patience, an authentic interest in his fellow citizens, and a sense of wonder and delight regarding the world we share. His main interest, it seemed, was to put a spotlight on others, not talk about himself. He seemed to revel in our diversity as human beings and yet focus on what we had in common. He celebrated the unique gifts of each person as well as what we all could contribute to the greater good.

One day while watching his show, as he was singing one of his iconic songs, "Tree Tree Tree," I became emotional. Perhaps it was because I love nature so much, but I suddenly felt a deep connection to his message. I finally understood why we need more people like Fred Rogers. As our social fabric and family lives have eroded, he has remained the steady man at the helm, helping children to cope and weather the storm. His calm demeanor and uplifting messages worked on my spirit, too.

I had never expected that to happen.

That afternoon, I made the decision to write him a letter of thanks. I had never written to anyone famous in my life, but I went upstairs while my daughter napped and penned a letter to him. In it, I thanked him for the wonderful role model he had been for children, especially for boys, and relayed that I appreciated his quiet, gentle, and calm way of talking to kids. I told him how much I valued the unhurried, happy place he created for children every day and thanked him for his life of service. I put my letter in the mailbox and did not give it much more thought after that.

Several months later, I opened my mailbox to find a large manilla envelope from *Mr. Rogers' Neighborhood*. Inside were two letters: one for me and one for my daughter. Mr. Rogers was known for writing his own letters to fans, answering thousands of them personally.

Dear Ms. Kolze,

It was very thoughtful of you to take the time to write and share with us some of your thoughts and feelings about our work. We're grateful to know our Neighborhood is a part of your daughter's growing up and that you have such good feelings about what she experiences with us.

All of us here are grateful for your warm appreciation for our Neighbors and for your caring comments about the "joy and sense of calm" you feel our program offers to children growing up in today's society. It also meant a great deal to me to know you feel we're offering positive role models for the boys who watch our program. The deep understanding and support of friends like you is an inspiration to all of us here.

It may interest you to know we are very much aware that the children who seem to like our Neighborhood best are the ones who have already experienced the deep investment of love in their own families, and so they are able to understand what we offer. I think this is particularly true with very young children like your daughter who respond so enthusiastically because of the warmth and love they feel in their own family relationships. Your child is fortunate to be growing up in such a caring family.

We're glad to send a letter and a Neighborhood postcard for your daughter, along with our best wishes for your family. We will remember with great pleasure that the Kolzes are a part of our Neighborhood...and that we're a part of yours.

Sincerely,

Fred Rogers

March 1999

Dear Ms. Kolze:

It was very thoughtful of you to take the time to write and share with us some of your thoughts and feelings about our work. We're grateful to know our Neighborhood is a part of your daughter's growing up and you have such good feelings about what she experiences with us.

All of us here are grateful for your warm appreciation for our Neighbors and for your caring comments about the "sense of joy and calm" you feel our program offers to children growing up in today's society. It also meant a great deal to me to know you feel we are offering positive role models for the boys that watch the program. The deep understanding and support from friends like you is an inspiration to all of us here.

It may interest you to know we are very much aware that the children who seem to like our Neighborhood best are the ones you have already experienced the deep investment of love in their own families, and so they are able to understand what we offer. I think this is especially true with very young children like your daughter who respond so enthusiastically because of the warmth and love they feel in their own family relationships. Your child is fortunate to be growing up in such a caring family. We will remember with great pleasure that the Kolzes are part of our Neighborhood . . . and that we're a part of yours.

Sincerely,
Fred Rogers[20]

Even someone as grounded and humble as Fred Rogers appreciated a compliment now and then. The envelope carrying the letter also included postcards of Daniel Tiger, the Trolley, King Friday, and the rest of the puppet cast. I knew immediately that I had made the right decision to reach out to this remarkable man. Today, these two letters are among my most prized possessions, carefully archived in my daughter's childhood scrapbook.

Sometimes it pays to take a risk and reach out to the people we value and appreciate—someone you might not necessarily even know personally. Writing to Fred Rogers helped me to process and articulate what I value most in people and relationships. A letter provides the perfect medium for this kind of exchange. Had I met him in person, I would have likely been tongue-tied, unable to deliver my heartfelt message.

What do we stand to lose? We owe it to each other to express gratitude for what we each do well in the world—especially when being our authentic selves means receiving harsh judgments or ridicule from some. These are the heroes in our midst.

By watching *Mr. Rogers' Neighborhood* and taking part in a brief exchange of letters, I became more certain of the need to show gratitude and appreciation for those we admire. Fred Rogers not only told us to be grateful for each other and the earth we live on, he walked the talk himself. By doing so, he quietly set a high bar that made others want to reach it, too.

Thank you, Fred Rogers, from the bottom of my heart.

Old Letters Reveal Our Core Truths

During the fall of 1985, when I helped my grandmother write her short autobiography, she talked to me about her first marriage to my grandfather, whom we called Pappy. She had saved some of the love letters he'd written as far back as the 1920s during their courtship.

That surprised me because my grandparents had divorced in the 1940s.

Grandma asked me to go into her antique oak secretary and retrieve these letters from the bottom shelf. In the dark, back-left corner, I found a tidy bundle of letters with lovely cursive writing on each of them, addressed to her. Because her eyesight was so poor at that point in her life, she asked me to read some of them to her.

Grandma lay down on her red-and-green floral couch. She put her hand dreamily to her forehead, closed her eyes, and listened carefully as I read several of his love letters out loud. It seemed like I was venturing into very private territory, so I stopped for a moment. She told me to continue, so I kept reading. At times, her face looked solemn, then changed to perplexed or analytical.

She was seeing their very old relationship through the wisdom she had gained from many more years of living and some self-reflection. As I remember them now, many years later, Pappy's letters included some rather flowery, romantic prose and expressions of love. I remember being surprised by his style of writing because my grandfather was an introverted, intellectual, socially awkward man in certain ways. Who would have thought that he had one romantic bone in his body? He was not what I thought of as a "warm and fuzzy" character.

Keeping old letters becomes especially important if we come from a family of introverts as I did—those who are sometimes reluctant to use their words and who are more private than others. Letters provide a new and different perspective on the people we think we know. Had I never read those letters, I would not be able to even imagine what attracted my grandparents to each other in the first place. Reading his personal diaries in recent years added yet another layer to my understanding of who my grandfather was.

We think we know people because of what we see with our eyes. But that is usually a simplistic and one-dimensional understanding of who someone is at their core. Letters can shine a light on the unseen still waters beneath the surface of our public personas.

I wonder how many people have been, or will be, harshly judged by history because we have not been able to fully know them as the colorful, beautiful, complicated, and flawed beings they are. If we better understood the feelings and motivations of the people we love, perhaps we could find the capacity to forgive them for their imperfections and decisions. We might be less likely to hang on to incorrect assumptions and unrealistic expectations, or take anger to our graves.

Reading old letters is one way to discover the whole truth of who we are as well of those we hold close or who may have deeply influenced us. We might be surprised to discover that Great-Aunt Edith swore like a sailor, that Uncle Bertie was a gambler, that your great-grandparents had to elope because of an unexpected pregnancy, and so on. There is one thing that letters make perfectly clear: we are all a very colorful and sometimes unpredictable lot, indeed.

Letters: Our Accidental Memoirs

My mother had a memory like a steel trap. She was a good storyteller because she could remember so many details about any event, circumstance, trip, or special place she had been. What always amazed me was the way she could tell the same story many times over the years and recite it with a nearly identical cadence and rhythm, incorporating the same descriptions and emotions. I could never master this kind of storytelling. I was never much good at details unless I *had* to be or because something really mattered or interested me. Each time I tell a story, I tend to focus on different details and am somewhat inconsistent in the way I tell it. There was a real difference in how my mother and I remembered things, because she was a detail person, and I most definitely am not.

Over the years, I have learned to help my memory along by taking notes, keeping journals, lists, and the like. Thank God that I started this practice early in my life. The truth is, without all that documentation, odd bits of my life history, like my interactions with a drunken truck driver who traveled with a pet python in his jacket, would forever be lost in the recesses of my mind, perhaps never shared with friends around a campfire. Fortunately, all your brain needs is a bit of a nudge, and the memories of people and places come flooding back.

Around the time my children were born, I met an older mother who encouraged me to keep a journal of my daughter's and son's early years because, she said, you will be sleep-deprived and busy, and will quickly forget their first words, the moment when they took their first steps, and many other wonderful milestones.

Really? How could I forget the most important times of my life? Because of youthful arrogance—that's how! I am so glad I decided to take this wise mother's words to heart, because as it turned out, she was 100 percent correct.

Now as I read my children's baby books and the journals I kept for them, I realize that I would have probably forgotten so many of the details of their development and many of the sweet things they said. Without my journals, I could never have recalled all the hilarity, joy, stress, fear, disgust, bliss, impatience that made parenting such a soulful experience. Because many of us are forgetful creatures, we need written documentation to help us remember, and here is another way that letters can help us. It turns out that for some of us, letters create an accidental record of our lives.

Returned to Sender

Away from home for many years, I often worried that my grandparents would feel isolated or lonely as they moved through their eighties, so I wrote to them on a fairly regular basis during my twenties and thirties. A great deal happened to me during those busy years: I went to college, I traveled abroad twice, had boyfriends, went to graduate school, got my first professional job, got married, and more. Much more. My letters to Grandma and her second husband, Reuben, captured many of these experiences in a raw and unedited fashion, just as I might have written about them in a diary or journal.

Many years after my grandmother died, I found out that she had kept all the letters from her grandchildren. My letters to her were subsequently given to my father for safekeeping. He in turn returned them to me before he died. At the time I wrote them, I never would have imagined that my letters would find their way back into my hands decades later.

The letters were a meaningful gift (I'm sure my grandmother knew it would be) because they sparked many memories as well as offered new insights into my youthful self. My "accidental memoir" reminds me that though my hair is now beginning to gray, I am still fundamentally the same person I always was, albeit a bit more cynical, worldly, and grateful than I was in my youth.

Several years ago, I visited a dear friend I have known since junior high school. I had been going through my own box of letters and found several from him when he lived in Miami at least thirty years ago. I decided to bring them along on a visit to his Chicago home. He read them out loud as we sat at his dining table sipping wine. While his addresses, jobs, and relationships changed many times, his basic values and perspectives had not really changed that much.

Recently, he returned the favor by presenting a Christmas card I had sent to him nearly forty years ago. In it, I described, in some detail, the man who would be my future husband. It was interesting to see that my earliest impressions proved true and my instincts about his character were spot on.

Rereading a letter you wrote long ago can be as exciting as opening a letter found in a bottle you discovered on a beach. As you unfold the yellowed paper, you are about to discover wonderful things about your young self as you ponder:

Was I honest and authentic as I wrote this letter?

Have I changed how I interpret the world around me?

How well did I know myself then?

Did this letter represent only the part of me that I felt safe sharing with others?

For my friend and me, the essence of our young selves is there on paper, and the letters' contents still ring true to us as we reread them so many years later. Old letters, written from the heart, don't lie or pretend. They merely hold onto the details we likely would have lost or decided to forget in the dusty corners of our minds.

For some, it can be oddly comforting to look back over a lifetime through the lens of old letters. For others, it might dredge up difficult memories. In either case, few things can capture the trivial, mundane, difficult, and memorable moments of our lives in the honest ways a letter can. And few things, save a diary or journal, allow us to look at the arc of our lives in this unvarnished way. It turns out that our younger selves have quite a bit to teach our older selves. Accidental memoirs allow us to take a sentimental look backward, while helping us to live out the remainder of our days based on the fruits of our self-reflection.

Old Letters Can Support Us in the Present

The COVID-19 pandemic has led people to search through their own family letters to learn more about how people survived the 1918 global pandemic. Many found a degree of comfort from their ancestors' words because they, like millions of other people, *did* survive that terrifying virus, just as most of us have today.

Old letters let us know that the human race is capable of facing countless adversities, including plagues, locusts, illness, childbirth, war, famine, poverty, and more. Passing on our experiences—including great challenges—in letters keeps an important record of our resiliency and our ability to continue to face into the winds of change and loss.

A "Flowery Letter" Never Forgotten

Some gifts are simple yet never forgotten; their impacts can ripple out in unforeseen ways.

My grandma Grace shared this story with me in her mid-eighties as I helped her write her autobiography for family members. The story is a testament to the power of maintaining caring connections and friendships through regular correspondence and reciprocal giving. It speaks to the importance of the little things we do that impact others in ways we often cannot imagine at the time.

My grandmother's family did not have much in the way of material wealth, so simple belongings and kind gestures were appreciated, remembered, and treasured.

Grandma Grace was one of nine children, the daughter of a Methodist preacher. In those days, the church required her father to move to a new parish every two to five years. You can imagine the amount of disruption this must have brought to this large and busy family, and she had to leave many friends behind. But she did her best to stay connected with some of them through letters.

My grandmother, Grace, among the flowers.

Most of the towns Grandma lived in were surrounded by prairie, wetlands, and other wild areas where she and her siblings could roam. It was in these small towns that my grandmother fell in love with nature and especially wildflowers. She adored flowers of all kinds and always had a small garden wherever she lived. I never remember visiting her house when she did not have a modest yet cheerful floral centerpiece on her dining room table.

In 1919, Grandma's family moved to Chicago. Once settled in the concrete jungle of the city, Grandma yearned for the places she had left behind. She would later tell me, "I longed for open spaces, the trees, and flowers. In the summer, the only flowers on our block were goldenrod, and even though the flowers were nothing special, I so envied their owners."

A friend she had left behind in Chatsworth, Illinois, understood, so she took it upon herself to plan a sweet surprise for her city friend. My grandmother described it to me this way, some seventy years later: "Several times over one summer, along with her usual letter, she sent me the most wonderful gift. She would take an old shoebox, line it with waxed paper, fill it with flowers, and sprinkle them with water. A certain train would leave Chatsworth each day and arrive in Chicago in time for our postal delivery the next morning. Even though the flowers would spend a day on the train, they would stay remarkably fresh. I just loved opening those boxes."

Several things about this story have remained with me. First, it surprised me that when sorting through her lifetime of experiences, my grandmother specifically wanted to tell me about this simple act of kindness by her friend and pen pal nearly seventy years earlier. It was also a reminder of how much people appreciate the small kindnesses done for them. Her friend's efforts to bring a bit of nature's beauty into my grandmother's city home obviously touched my grandmother. Perhaps this generosity served as a model for the many kind things my grandmother did for her own friends, children, and grandchildren in subsequent years. She sometimes gave small gifts or created small occasions "just because." It was her way of paying it forward, just as her friend in Chatsworth had done for her.

It doesn't take much to make someone's day. Simple gifts—a special letter, a card, a handmade gift—that often cost us little to nothing can be remembered for a lifetime. After all, a shoebox full of wildflowers was the best kind of gift my grandmother could receive.

Perhaps it was the stories of these special offerings that encouraged me to similarly invest my time and energy in writing letters. In due course, that gift for my grandmother rippled out through her to me and in turn to many of my own friends and family members.

You might want to chalk up this story to times gone by, to a behavior we will not see again. I beg to differ. Times change—your loved ones do not. So make a similar loving gesture to someone you know, just for the joy it might bring them. Cards and letters, with or without flowers, are great places to start. Who knows? One hundred years from now, they may be telling someone about the wonderful gift *you* gave them at an important time in their life—that special thing *you* sent that touched their heart.

Letters We Remember

A Letter to You

Writing myself to you
it is simple
I am just writing myself
in blue—
an inky hand
where colors tell of many
moods all true

Line leads to line
quite simply
as line leads to line
I croon
my truths, my bequests
creations, behests
without necessarily score or tune
unless
if what I have written
seems simple
as you read what I have written to show
steadfast or with tremor or shiver in
the letters of the letter you'll know

More than characters
to what score I have written, then
not just words I have
penned to a line to yearn,
but a letter to you from my heart —
now to you
so that of me you will learn
as I may of you upon your loved heart's
written return.

—Julie Kolze Sorensen

Thank-You Letters: Why Showing Appreciation Never Goes Out of Style

Cultivate the habit of being grateful for every good thing that comes to you and give thanks continuously. And because all things have contributed to your advancement, you should include all things in your gratitude.

—Ralph Waldo Emerson

Thank you. Two simple words.

Yet the thank-you note seems less and less common these days, though the need for it has never gone away, nor will it ever go out of fashion. Showing gratitude for the kindness and generosity of others is one of the most important social conventions we have. Why? Because thank-you cards and letters acknowledge and show our understanding that the person who gave you their valuable time, thought, money, and caring in the form of a gift *did not have to do it*. In our increasingly busy world, when time is precious to everyone and there are dozens of tasks on each of our to-do lists, showing our appreciation with a handwritten thank-you card or letter is more important than ever.

Accepted social rules and behaviors vary according to the times we live in. However, most of the social conventions of the day are ideals embedded in the Golden Rule: do unto others as you would have them do unto you. Showing appreciation and expressing gratitude are simply appropriate, often expected, and always valued by the person who gives a gift. Not taking the time to acknowledge someone's generosity shows a sense of entitlement.

By the time my children came along, I had already noticed a decline in the use of thank-you notes, so I encouraged my son and daughter to make showing appreciation a priority. Sure, I had to remind them many times during their formative years; however, I am pleased that, as adults, they have incorporated gratitude and thank-you notes into their own lives automatically.

Not only is the thank-you letter an important social convention and kind offering, it can also make you feel good as well. Many studies that suggest that the practice of demonstrating gratitude is good for us. An earlier chapter in this book entitled, "Skip the Gym: Why Letter Writing Is Good for Us" discusses the health benefits of outwardly showing our appreciation for the efforts of others. In fact, people who practice gratitude on a regular basis exhibit increased satisfaction with relationships and fewer symptoms of physical illness, view their lives less materialistically than others, and suffer less envy than people who do not think much about it.[21]

"Gratitude has one of the strongest links to mental health, more so than even optimism. Benefits can be lifelong. A sense of gratitude can reduce the lifetime risk of depression, anxiety, and substance abuse," says psychologist Dr. Shilagh Mirgain.[22] While no one gives a gift just to receive a thank-you note, our willingness to take a few moments to acknowledge and show appreciation for the dedication of someone's time and effort on our behalf is a win-win for all involved.

The words *please* and *thank you* are deeply important expressions that should come from a sincere and authentic place. Sending a thank-you note is still a wonderful and important gesture, even if you have expressed your appreciation in person. Should you forget to write that important thank-you note on one occasion, the giver will likely forgive you with ease. However, if we repeatedly fail to acknowledge their generosity, we shouldn't be surprised if, on our next birthday, graduation, or special occasion, we become the forgotten ones.

Giving to others and receiving thanks for your generosity are part of a satisfying reciprocal process that has existed for thousands of years. So, please, give thanks when it's appropriate—commit your own true feelings to paper—and ensure that giving gifts and receiving thanks remain a shared, cyclical process we can all feel good about.

And, for your efforts, thank you very much.

Gratitude Letters: Beyond the Simple Thank-You

I would maintain that thanks are the highest form of thought, and that gratitude is happiness doubled by wonder.

—G. K. Chesterton

The only thing I ever wanted to be was a public servant. I had a calling—I wanted to try to make a difference in protecting water quality in lakes, rivers, and streams. And so, for more than three decades, I worked in state and federal government agencies doing just that. By and large, my colleagues were delightful to work with, and I admired them for their dedication, knowledge, tenacity, and the sense of purpose they brought to their work. Most had trained for years to work in their chosen professional fields—chemistry, biology, engineering, public policy—and they cared deeply about the natural world.

I often wished that the public had a better understanding of their level of commitment. A great deal of effort and expertise is involved in ensuring that the public has safe water to drink and that sewage is adequately treated before being discharged back into our favorite lakes and rivers.

Many public servants deserve sincere appreciation rather than ire from the public they serve. Their own managers and supervisors could often show greater appreciation as well. I often thought how easy it would have been to change this dynamic and their morale at the same time. All it would have taken is a few kind words regularly given for work well done. Sentiments like "Thank you for choosing public service," "Thank you for deciding to work here and for the great service you give!" "We are so lucky to have you," or "You have done a terrific job, once again" would be so easy to say and cost nothing at all. Appreciation, expressed face-to-face, often means more to people than simple monetary rewards.

It doesn't seem much different in the private sector. I often heard similar stories from friends about the lack of positive verbal feedback from their supervisors and managers. One colleague in a local Toastmasters club I once belonged to was fortunate enough to have received a handwritten note from his supervisor, which had praised him for his consistent good work. My colleague had kept that note card tucked inside the pocket of his office binder for some time. We both agreed in unison that an email "would never be the same." It took such a small amount of effort on the part of this supervisor to recognize and reward the great skills and value this professional brought to the company each day. The impact of this handwritten note was priceless.

From the many articles I have read in the *Harvard Business Review* over the years, it appears that many managers and supervisors fail to regularly express appreciation to their staff for a job well done. And I think it is safe to say that most people do not give or receive enough praise and recognition *in general*, whether at home, at school, at work, or at play.

Yet we should endeavor to show our gratitude more often, since research has shown that grateful people, as well as those who feel appreciated, are much more engaged with their environment, experience greater personal growth and self-acceptance, and have stronger feelings of purpose, meaning, and satisfaction in their lives.[23]

Why Is Gratitude Difficult to Share?

Research presents complex reasons why some people struggle more with expressing gratitude than others. There appears to be both nature (genetic) and nurture (family and life experience) elements at play here.[24] Personality traits and values can act as barriers to gratitude. Envy, insecurities, materialism, narcissism, and cynicism can make it difficult to feel or express gratitude. Many people experience life through a scarcity mindset, thinking only about what they don't have rather than feeling grateful for what they do have.[25] Whether it is nature, nurture, or both, Dr. Neel Burton believes that our general inclination as human beings is to struggle with the notion of expressing gratitude to others.[26]

But research also suggests that we can exercise our gratitude "muscle" and increase our capacity to express love and thankfulness either by creating a gratitude journal or writing gratitude letters.

In his inspiring book *365 Thank Yous: The Year a Simple Act of Daily Gratitude Changed My Life*, author John Kralik describes the transformative experience he had when he handwrote a thank-you note to someone different each day for a year. As he developed his ability to show gratitude for the people and experiences in his life, amazing blessings began to appear that would help to turn around what he describes as "a life in the dumps."

It's Never Too Late to Say Thank You

My mother was very private about her thoughts and emotions, yet she knew it was important to let people know why she valued and loved them, so she worked at being more open with her feelings. For example, around the time of her father's eighty-fifth birthday, she sat down one day and wrote this much-beloved man a letter of gratitude—one of the most meaningful gifts she would ever give him. She most likely had been thinking about writing this letter for quite a long time but, like most of us, was distracted by her busy life. For me, her letter is a wonderful example of what a gratitude letter should convey: a deep appreciation for the many ways in which the person to which we are writing has touched our lives and been important to our own development as a person.

Her father, my grandfather, was not a perfect man. However, he was remarkable in so many ways. Here are the words my mother wrote to her father on that special occasion:

> Dearest Daddy,
>
> I wanted to write this letter to you a couple of weeks or more ago, before the occasion of your 85th birthday . . . .
>
> Before your birthday, I did a lot of thinking about how lucky I have always been to have had you and Mother as parents, and although, sadly for both of us, she is now gone—I still have you. We're all so happy that you achieved the age of 85 so we could enjoy having you with us for so many more years, and we hope there will be many more "happy birthdays" for you to celebrate.
>
> I have always admired so much the courage and optimism with which you faced life, for you could much more easily have taken a negative approach or given up in the face of sickness and hardship. Instead, you chose a positive outlook—thankful for life and the chance to enjoy it, always striving to make the best of any situation, and always looking for the best in people. One of the nicest things is that you have never lost your sense of humor. Too often, in many people, this quality disappears with age.

I am sure that through your life you have been an inspiration to many—certainly me—and in various ways you have had a positive effect on all the family. Your many friends have all been profoundly touched by your life, and this is shown in the ways they remember you. As your friend wrote in his Christmas card to you, "After all, it is not the big things one does in life, but all the little things done out of love for people all your life through, that count the most."

Again, happy birthday! I love you very much and am proud to be your daughter.

— Natalie

My mother and her father, Jonah,
around the time she wrote him this letter.

Can you imagine how my grandfather must have felt reading my mother's words? I'm sure they affected him deeply. And we have proof that it was a treasured possession, since it was one of but a few letters my grandfather had saved in an old shoebox on the shelf of his closet. And years later, when I read my mother's letter to her father for the first time, I had a much deeper understanding of the person she was, as well as the level of admiration and love she had for her father.

It took her fifty years to express these heartfelt sentiments. Fortunately, he lived long enough to read them.

My own father was also a sensitive man who worked hard in his later years to tell his children and relatives how he felt about them. His preferred mode, just like my mother's, was to put his feelings in writing. In the last years of his life, he wrote me the following in my birthday card:

> Happy Birthday, Dear Lynne! You are a lady of great accomplishments, of which I am so proud. All of them done with loving care, for your family and friends, and the great world we live in. I hope this will be a very special day for a very special person. Thank you for all the help.
>
> Much love, Dad

It does not take much effort to totally transform someone's day—or even to change a life. Loving words of gratitude whether spoken or written can give each of us this needed sustenance—like the drops of rain that refresh or sustain a garden. Those who share these precious words with us nurture lives. They model love in ways that we can follow, creating ripple effects that cannot be quantified.

Gratitude, Just Because

You don't need to wait for a momentous occasion or write a long, involved letter of gratitude. Sometimes a short note that says "Thanks for your help" or "I am grateful to have you as a friend (or colleague, boss)" on a pretty card has deep meaning to the recipient. How about a letter or card for the mail carrier, your children's teachers, a hairstylist, revealing how much you appreciate all that they do every day to make the world a better place?

A respondent to my informal letters survey shared a touching message about the powerful impact a gratitude letter had on her life: "I got a letter from a friend that was bipolar . . . She thanked me for always having time for her, told me how wonderful I am, how grateful she was for her life and me. Her life was so hard. I was very humbled by the letter—made my problems seem small. Felt foolish for ever complaining. I read it when I need a lift. I keep it nearby."

My sister's friend shared another lovely example of a short note imbued with gratitude. She received this note from a woman friend, now passed away, whom she had met at college: "Doesn't the picture on this card remind you of the two of us sipping Russian tea? Monday was such a delightful day. Of course, any time when I am with you is special for me . . . All in all, it was a wonderful day. Thank you so much for inviting me. Fondly, L."

Letter writing at its most basic level shows gratitude for the recipient because by taking the time to create a letter, we are showing others that we deeply value the connection with them.

Write a Letter, Change a Life

After hearing people's stories for more than sixty years, I can truthfully say that not everyone is fortunate when it comes to having a caring family or devoted friends. If you are one of the lucky ones, consider thanking the universe for your own good fortune.

Few people experience true, unconditional love. If we are lucky enough to know that kind of love, we can help someone else to experience it as well. Consider telling someone you admire how they have helped you become the person you are and why it matters that they have been part of your life. Explain what it is about them that you value and how you have tried to incorporate what they model into your own life. Write whatever comes from the heart. Send it sooner rather than later. None of us ever want to regret what we should have said or written but never did. Closing the circle of love with a card or letter is a gift of the highest order and, at the same time, one of the greatest gifts we could ever give ourselves.

Letters from Our Grandmothers

"I'll never throw away any of the letters my grandmother sent me," my hairstylist told me one day. I have heard this sentiment often. Letters from our grandmothers are often some of the most treasured possessions we own. Putting them in the trash is unthinkable. Our deep attachment to them isn't surprising, because they often represent the unconditional love grandparents give us—the kind of acceptance we don't always find as easily from other people in our lives. Through their consistent and loving presence, grandmothers are often our greatest supporters and the glue that holds far-flung families together.

My grandmother Grace understood the importance of our spending time together, of sharing a meal and a lively conversation. She savored the times when people would leave their busy lives behind and become wholly present with one another around her kitchen table. She invested deeply in her role as matriarch, ensuring that family get-togethers happened with regularity and that they reflected her brand of hospitality and fun. Family was the center of her world, and as her grandchildren, we felt that in our bones.

Her welcoming home, in a quaint Chicago suburb, had simple furnishings and the art she could afford. Upon entering her home, your focus was not on the quality of the furniture or carpeting but instead on your invitation to the table, to a conversation, and to her undivided attention. Her home was a soft place to land, a place to get a good meal and an endless cup of coffee, no matter the hour.

Each summer during my youth, my brother and I would stay at my grandmother's house for three or four days at a time. The town was home to a small, private college, many Victorian homes, and quiet, leafy streets. Our visits there always seemed to fall during the hottest dog days of summer.

I look back fondly on these times when my grandmother made us slow down and spend meaningful time together. During our annual visits, she would usually encourage us to create art, play board games and croquet, exchange corny jokes, talk about school and friends, and get to know something about our family heritage, one person and one story at a time. Old photo albums that we frequently looked through helped us connect her stories to faces and places. Her stories grounded me and gave me a sense of belonging in my large extended family.

At Grandma's house, solo activities were frowned upon. It was in her home that I learned what the term *convivial* meant: the warm exchanges and laughter that always found its way into mealtime conversations. There was a sense of safety and contentment because in this place, we always knew we were loved and accepted, just as we were.

Later, when I left my parents' nest and went off to college and my first professional jobs, letters between my grandmother and me became an extension of what we had experienced in her sunny, yellow kitchen around the old oak table. Her letters were warm, chatty, conversational. She would share the names of recent visitors, the weather, favorite TV shows, the books she and Reuben, my step-grandfather, were reading, the plants blooming in the garden—and what I remember most vividly was her advice on how to stay healthy.

In her later years, her letters became more philosophical. She wrote about her religious beliefs, the importance of education, the value of finding one's purpose in life. The best letters conjure the writer's voice and manner, and Grandma's did this well. Here are a few excerpts from some of her wonderful letters.

ON OUR PURPOSE HERE

April 25, 1982

You have a noble purpose (government service), and you will be helped by a higher power, if you trust. It is hard to understand, but it is so. There is much in life that we do not understand—we use energies every day that we do not understand. There are mental and spiritual energies available to all who have a sincere heart. Especially if these energies are to be used for the development of talent and for service to others.

ON APPRECIATION

March 8, 1982

One of the nicest surprises on my birthday was your thoughtful and very generous letter. It really added a certain joy to everything. To know that I have added a bit to your store of memories was happiness indeed. You have made me feel like the richest woman in Naperville because you have given me such a rich store myself and made my life so very full. Your letter was the most rewarding gift you could have given me. It is a fine quality—your gift of appreciation. That you also take the time and effort to let it be known is much appreciated by me.

ON OUR PURPOSE IN LIFE

March 8, 1982

Sometimes, unexpected things just happen in life that make it necessary to change one's dreams and plans, and we find ourselves in unexpected circumstances. All we can do is to "bend with the wind" and do the best we can—and it may be far from our dreams. I believe that God loves each of us with an infinite love and gently guides our lives, though we might not be aware of it. Through big and little decisions, we try to make the most of our lives. The "most" may happen to be a humble service in humble circumstances. The gift of life should not be taken lightly. Each individual is responsible to do the best possible with such a gift, or otherwise great potential could be wasted.

ON INTERGENERATIONAL SHARING

August 31, 1981

We miss you. Especially today it seems important, helpful, and pleasurable to be with young people who are active, and ambitious and purposeful. These are things limited in later years, so being able to hear and share with young people is great. Perhaps this is one of the blessings of the family unit. Without it, different ages of people would not naturally be thrown together. People would probably only be grouped with their peers (which is already happening in retirement homes) instead of family units, where nature brings together sometimes 2 or 3 generations.

ON THE CREATOR

January 3, 1992

Here are a few lines I have put together for my Christmas message. "We accept the mysteries of life in humility, trusting in the wisdom and love of the Creator to sustain us."

ON TEMPTATION

February 5, 1992

You are really helping us to stay sweet! What fun to get a package in the mail, struggling a half hour to open it, and then finding such a gorgeous box of treats! What luck at 89! We are truly in the lap of luxury! We both love chocolates, and in my association with Reuben (over 25 years now), I have never seen him turn one down (in fact, he steals one, occasionally. I have caught him!)

The most memorable parts of her letters, of course, are the loving affirmations she constantly gave me that buoyed me up and helped me to believe in myself. These are treasured words I could never discard. There, on now-yellowed paper, her words remind me that giving and being grateful are circular and infinite, that just a few minutes spent devoted to someone else could change a life, that our everyday acts of helping and caring might be remembered by someone their whole life through.

In her late eighties, when her eyes failed her, Grandma hired a helper to whom she could dictate letters. These letters would always arrive in easy-to-read cursive. At that point, it was a bit of a relief, because her sentences crisscrossed and overlapped each other on the page, and the fat black marker she used made the letters blur together in a tangled mess. Yet no matter how hard it became to read her letters, I spent the time trying, mostly because I knew how much this kind of communication meant to her and it was a great effort for her to write these letters to me.

I am so grateful to have had a grandmother who took an interest in my boyfriends, travels, academic achievements, and general disappointments. In her letters, she never failed to offer gentle support and encouragement.

When I reread her letters today, it is as if she and I are sitting at her kitchen table having a cup of coffee together, telling stories and being completely present in that moment of sharing. I can no longer be with her, so her letters are the next best thing. I treasure them.

The Universal Power of a Grandmother's Love

As I write this chapter, I am sitting at Grandma's old oak table, many miles from her old home. It is a special possession, now out of style, but which will remain with me forever. It will always remind me of what she modeled: that the most important things in life are often free. That central to the best of times are focused, joyful conversations and being truly present for one another. For my grandmother, conversation was key to creating and sustaining any relationship.

And the best way to communicate was in person, if possible. Letters and phone calls were second-best.

In the middle of writing this chapter, I experienced an interesting coincidence.

With my hair washed and wrapped in a towel, I sat back in the hair salon chair. A new, young hairstylist named Kaleigh carefully placed a black cape around me. As she wielded her scissors, we began to chat. I enjoy these opportunities to get to know people much younger than myself, so I began to ask questions.

Kaleigh is a twenty-year-old woman with a round face, curly hair, and authentic smile. The conversation soon turned to the work I do. I explained my desire to write a book about letters and how we could resurrect the practice of writing them to the people we love. Her face perked up.

"I agree," she said. "I write letters all the time. I love letters!"

I must admit, I was surprised. I tend to think of letter writers as a bunch of aging, eccentric romantics from older generations.

"Look!" she said. She turned her arm toward my face. On the underside of her left arm, above the wrist, was a tattoo. It was not a picture. Instead, it consisted of a few lines of elegant cursive lettering that read "Love you, Kaleigh. Grandma Q."

It turned out that these exact words of love, in this precise cursive, were from Kaleigh's baptism card her Grandma Q. wrote many years before. This grandmother has since died, but she left Kaleigh the legacy of a special card and simple words of love to remember her by. It was clear by the way Kaleigh talked about her grandmother that she loved her deeply—so much so that she took this special card to a tattoo salon where it was scanned into a computer and developed into a stencil for her tattoo. An exact replica of Grandma Q.'s handwriting will be with her forever, always available to cheer her each day.

Grandfathers Matter, Too

I do not wish to slight the loving grandfathers out there who faithfully write letters to their grandchildren. In preparation for writing this book, I conducted a small, unscientific survey of letter enthusiasts. One of the respondents spoke of a letter she received from her grandfather during her early adulthood. Her story proves that a simple card or letter can indeed change a life:

"There was a letter from my grandpa when I was in college—a beautiful written letter letting me know that I can be whatever I want to be."

Another respondent recalls: "My grandfather lived in Montreal in the later part of his life. We met in person only a handful of times, but we exchanged letters almost weekly for many years. This turned out to be a very important relationship for me during my formative years. I kept every single letter he sent me and love knowing that they exist and that I can look back on them at any time."

Grandparents can often share wisdom, experience, and love in a way that parents cannot. And grandparents seem more capable of loving us unconditionally than others, providing the anchor we need when things in life become chaotic. Their houses can be places of relaxation and comfort during the turbulent or dark times of our lives. When we are tempted to judge ourselves harshly, their constant and unwavering love can help us to tame or ignore our darkest thoughts.

Grandparents often model what we already know: that high-touch, low-tech interactions matter. That a short, personal note, a special letter, or visit are time-worthy activities and that these simple activities are precisely what we all need. They speak to our basic human needs to be seen, recognized, and loved, above all else.

Now Is the Time to Return the Favor

For those fortunate to have loving grandparents still in your lives, I encourage you to take a few moments out of your busy schedule to return the love and support you have received from them. Please consider writing them a quick card or letter of gratitude. One survey respondent took it a step further. She writes: "I once got a letter from my grandmother, who asked me to write more about my day-to-day life because she wanted to be able to picture it and know me better. I always wrote more in-depth letters about my everyday life to everyone after that, and my grandmother told me how much she loved knowing more about what I did on a regular basis."

If you should be lucky enough to receive your grandparents' letters in return, I suggest that you keep them. You and others will enjoy and cherish their letters long after they leave this earth.

Be Still My Heart: Long Live the Love Letter

In his book, *Wouldn't It Be Something*, Dennis Depcik writes beautifully of the exchange of love letters that brought him and his wife together, resulting in a marriage that lasted more than forty years. It started innocently enough: a teenage girl writing letters to her sister's brother-in-law, an army officer in training, during the Vietnam War. Despite the difference in their ages, they would go on to exchange more than a hundred letters during his time overseas.

As the years passed, they wrote to each other more frequently, and eventually, they fell in love for a lifetime through the letters they devotedly wrote to one another. Depcik writes: "Mary Brown continued to write, and I continued to answer, and in the course of writing to each other over three years, everything changed. Mary Brown became far more than just a kid. She became my life."[27]

In one letter from Mary to Dennis, she made an insightful comment about the power of letter writing: "It just occurred to me that if you were home, we would probably never really get to know each other as we have through our letters. We would be too busy having a good time or something. I don't want it to be like that, do you?"[28]

Writing a love letter takes time and intention. The act of sitting with your thoughts and writing a letter to the object of your affections requires you to be present and to give of yourself in a way that is quite selfless. A love letter should convey a real interest in and curiosity about your sweetheart's interests, activities, and feelings. And, just as importantly, it should communicate your deepest appreciation for the ways your lover has enriched your experiences and blessed your life. Even the best poets and authors in the world have struggled to find the right ways to express love. But it is important that we try to express these tender emotions.

The act of committing your romantic feelings to paper blends vulnerability with a twist of risk-taking. The author of a love letter is never quite sure how the object of their affection will react to such an open expression of their love.

In many cases, those who write love letters probably worry too much. Assuming there is a mutual chemistry between two people, the recipient will likely feel deeply touched by the attempt at the very least—and perhaps become more certain of their love for the author because of it.

The recipients of love letters are often willing to overlook spelling errors, the coffee stains on the paper, or the mismatched stationery. What matters most is the effort—the action to create something special, a one-of-a-kind gift intended for their eyes only. A respondent to my letters survey shares that "I had several romantic relationships over the years, and letters always got my heart beating a little stronger. An email or text in that regard would pale in comparison to a heartfelt note from a special someone."

Many of the women I know have kept love letters, even when they did not come from the men who became their husbands. Take, for instance, my friend who kept a special card she had received from an admirer, even after she was married to someone else. "For me," she says, "the handwritten word has such significance. It is as unique as the person who wrote it, and email will never be a substitute. Email is 'flat' and lifeless. For me, handwritten words are filled with life and the person's character. I don't know how many times in a life, if ever, a person receives such a beautifully written card or letter as I did. That is why I kept it."

Love letters, when written with sincerity and authentic emotion, can be surprisingly beautiful and lyrical, no matter who the author. Their heartfelt expressions will undoubtedly be remembered and reread for decades to come.

We All Need Love Letters

I am not alone in cherishing the love letter. Today's lifestyle encourages electronic connection, but for the most part, I believe women (and men) still deeply yearn for romantic gestures from their lovers. Letters are one of the most meaningful offerings of love we can receive.

A woman I surveyed writes about the few words her future husband penned that changed her life: "My husband and I fell in love writing letters and emails when we lived in different states. One letter had a huge impact on me. It came during a time before we were together, but when I had a big crush on him. The card had a photo of a beautiful misty lake and a colorful boat in the foreground, and he simply wrote inside: 'Grand adventures await us.' We bonded over our mutual love of travel. I looked at that card countless times and swooned over the idea of our future together."

Another person shares that her husband won her heart when he wrote a five-page letter telling her all the things he loved about her. In my view, it would take a good deal of effort to rebuff such an expression of love!

Take a Lesson from History

The love letter has been around for hundreds of years. There has been no end to the many ingenious ways people have used letters to initiate relationships. Perhaps their letter writing began as a slow burn—by exchanging updates on the weather, the price of corn, or with a description of the writer's trip to a county fair. All nice and polite. But then, with each subsequent letter, the writers slowly divulged new information or more complex feelings, turning their friendly pen pal relationship into something much more: an intimate and passionate love affair.

John and Abigail Adams ignited then kept their love light burning through an exchange of 1,100 letters that lasted nearly forty years.[29] Poet Robert Browning and his wife, Elizabeth Barrett, began their relationship first by exchanging pleasantries and talking of simple, polite news of the day. But with time, their letters became more intimate, culminating in a secret marriage.

What more can I say?

What We Are in Danger of Losing

It is a shame that in the age of technology, most people no longer send or receive handwritten love letters—even though, according to one survey, a whopping 70 percent of women would rather receive a poem or a love letter than some form of digital communication from a significant other.[30] These statistics tell me that many people in partnerships are secretly disappointed and silently longing for that elusive paper letter.

Carrying on a love affair via the internet seems one-dimensional and less satisfying. If virtual romance is working so well, why are there so many people longing for more tangible, analog forms of loving expression? If it is old-fashioned to desire a romantic love letter, then most women, it appears, are guilty as charged. Feminism and a desire for courtship and romance are not antithetical. Strong women, and men, too, appreciate the validation and caring that love letters demonstrate.

I am fortunate to have had parents who understood romance in life on many levels, and who, by living it, modeled the way for their children. Their courtship was romantic and loving, requiring little more than time together doing thoughtful and inexpensive things for one another. They were married for sixty-four years, and until the end, my father continued to woo my mother with handmade birthday and anniversary cards, and intentionally creating space for them to spend time together on the simple things they both enjoyed doing.

A love letter can be food for the soul for the recipient, a reassurance that they matter and are loved—especially important when we are at a distance from our lovers. Sometimes it can take a while for love to blossom. In my letters survey, one man writes, "I wrote letters back and forth to my first love back in Ohio. That was fifty years ago. We just got married this year."

Please do not hesitate to speak of your love for others. If the spoken words do not come easily to you, use pen and paper instead. But please consider doing one or the other. By taking this vulnerable first step, you will be closer to having a powerful and lasting relationship. As you write your letter of love, understand the rich and rewarding gift you are giving. With any luck, this loving gift will come back to you in a hundred splendid ways.

Love Letters for the Next Generation?

I was standing at the checkout counter at a grocery store, ready to buy some wine. I asked a young man behind the counter, "Do you still take checks here?"

His eyes lit up and he smiled. "Yes, I love taking checks. They are so retro!"

"Great!" I said, smiling. "I still love my checks. It's hard for me to give them up."

"Really?" he said quizzically. "Why do you like them so much?"

I had to think for a second. "I like the action of writing in cursive and the fact that I can see and touch the check. I suppose that is why

I also love to write letters," I added. "In fact, I am writing a book about handwritten letters."

At this point, I had his attention. His curiosity got the best of him. "A book about letters?" he asked, looking skeptically at me as he scrunched up his eyes.

"Yes," I said. "Have you ever written one?"

"No," he said.

Without hesitation and at the risk of being labeled "retro" myself, the words tumbled out of me. "I have to tell you that if you ever want to win the heart of someone you are crazy about, write them a letter—or many letters. They will be very touched. Not only that, but you will also make their entire month—or year! I have been doing some research on the love letter, and I can tell you that women still want and wish for them. My husband used to write me love letters, and I still have all of them. When I reread them, I am reminded of why I fell in love with him all those years ago."

"Really?" he said. "Love letters?"

"Yes," I replied. "I recently told my son that if he finds that right person, please write them love letters, please keep this wonderful tradition alive for the next generation."

At this point, he was all ears, completely focused on our conversation. "I am seriously taking mental notes on what you are saying—really. I am hearing you," he said, smiling.

"Wonderful," I replied, "because I am counting on you! Love letters are the most meaningful gift of all. And do not stop with your partner. Write one to your parents, siblings, or anyone else you care about. They will never, ever throw that letter away, and it will mean the world to them their whole lives through."

As I gathered up my purchase, he repeated to me in an earnest way, "I am going to give this some serious thought."

"Fantastic!" I said with a smile. "As I said, I am counting on you!"

While I understand how the computer has lured us away from writing by hand, I also grieve for what has gone with it. How many men with tender, romantic hearts wish they could simply share the full breadth of themselves with loved ones without the feeling that they must adhere to toxic expectations of what masculinity should be? The saddest part is that women and men too often do not set an expectation that they would like to be romanced, respected, and cherished in longer-term relationships. We are not likely to get what we need unless we ask for it.

When looking for a mate, forget the six-pack abs, fancy cars, or perfect model smiles. Instead, ask your crush, "Do you write love letters?" If they do, consider yourself very lucky to have found another romantic soul willing to work for your love. If your beloved uses words well and is willing to take their time to enjoy the process of falling in love slowly using the written word, it's likely that they have a great deal more to offer than meets the eye.

We Can Still Be Romantics in a Digital Age

During the early years of my husband's and my courtship, we were apart for months at a time, with him finishing his degree in Paris, and me back in Chicago waiting to secure my first professional job. Those months seemed to pass at a glacial pace, but my spirits remained high because of his wonderful, loving letters. These letters cemented us together as friends and lovers even more than our phone calls, because we shared memorable and difficult experiences we were having while apart.

My husband regularly wrote to me about his walks through the Paris neighborhoods, the unforgettable sights and sounds in the streets and markets, his visits to the famed bookstore Shakespeare and Company, his discovery of small, enchanting parks, as well as his thoughts about the classes and professors at the École Nationale d'Administration. Most meaningful to me, of course, were the ways in which he expressed his wish that I could be there with him, in one of the most romantic cities in the world.

I, on the other hand, would share more mundane, but important news about the trials and tribulations of trying to land my first federal job at the Environmental Protection Agency in Chicago, despite the

My husband's letters were always a delight during the times we were apart and are still treasured keepsakes.

threat of a national hiring freeze. Our letters created an intimacy and closeness that bridged the distance between us. They allowed us to give voice to feelings we may have never been able to articulate the same way in person.

The things that originally attracted me to my husband—the witty young man with a fountain pen, decades ago—still do today. His letters gave me a unique insight into the most important, subtle, loving, and passionate parts of him.

I fell in love with his soul.

The pen and paper are powerful tools for love and romance. I encourage you to write a love letter to your beloved in your own handwriting and in your own words. Help to keep this beautiful, sublime tradition from disappearing from our lives. It does not matter if your lover lives next door, across the country, or sleeps in your own bed. Writing your feelings with pen and paper will make your partner's day. Please, never underestimate how much the handwritten word means.

Someday in the future, your relatives may happen upon your letters, read them, and better understand the depths of your personality and your great capacity for love—the greatest legacy of all.

A Soldier's Letters Home

It is 1949. A nineteen-year-old man from the Midwest with a dream of being a professional photographer finds himself enlisting in the army in the years after World War II and before the Korean War. He knows they will draft him if he doesn't volunteer. He just wants to get it over with so he can get on with his life. His beautiful fiancée will be waiting for him when he completes his tour of duty. The couple is excited about getting married and beginning their life together when he returns to the States.

My father just before his tour of duty in Japan, 1949.

The young, enlisted man soon finds himself stationed in occupied Japan at US Army General Headquarters in Tokyo. When he enlists, he believes he will have a one-year commitment to Uncle Sam. Little does he know that he will be drafted for a second round of duty in 1950 during the Korean War, this time as an army photographer.

This young man was my father, Larry M. Kolze. My father was not what you would call a military enthusiast, but he did his duty as society expected of him at that time. He was an introvert, a sensitive man with the heart of an artist. He loved home and his family life far more than the military experience. Quoting a fellow soldier at the end of their tour of duty, he said, "I wouldn't take a million dollars for the experience I had, but I wouldn't take a million to go back in either."

During his time in the army, my father wrote letters home whenever he could find the time. Even though his mind was mostly focused on the woman he left behind (my mother), he took some care to keep his mother informed of what his life in the army was like. His letters to her are a window into the soul of a young man as he came to grips with his new reality:

> Mom, By the time you receive this letter, I will be on ship ready to pull out for Japan. It is a strange sensation knowing there is a home and loved ones behind you that you must leave for such a long time and at such a long distance. Our trip here (to California) was one of beauty, but that longing to be in the home state with your home people never leaves for a minute.

In soldiers' letters to their families, a deep yearning for home and the sense of normalcy it represented is a consistent theme. Many are unapologetically sweet and sentimental while maintaining a reassuring tone for mothers and fathers they left behind. And not knowing their fate from day to day, some soldiers no doubt were more willing to express themselves openly and honestly just in case it might be their last chance.

There were few things more important to a soldier than news from home. One infantryman, Paul Fusell, stated it clearly: "The mail was indispensable. It was terribly important as a motivator for troops. Mail call, whenever it happened, was a delight."[31]

The desire to hear from family members back home never seemed to diminish as the months and years of war went by. My mother-in-law's cousin, a Royal Air Force pilot during World War II, reminded her sister, Marion, to please send him mail three different times within the same letter, writing "Please write immediately" twice and "Tell your dad to please drop me a line if he gets some spare time" once. His letter is full of a longing for home—his desire to return to normal routines and to see family and friends.

As my father faced an unknown future and an ocean voyage that took him far from his humble home, he voiced his deepest gratitude to his mother:

> From all your letters it sounds as though everything is in good shape. That makes me very happy. I can't begin to tell you how much I miss you and wish I was home again, but there is little use in crying, for I am here, and here I will stay for a while.
>
> What I want most of all to tell you is I am well and that I do remember the love you have always shown me, and I hope that someday, I will be able to repay the many things you have done for me.
>
> Home sounds like an exciting place to me with the new puppies, Rita, Polly at work, and Susy working at the papers. You good people sound right happy and busy. Things seem so far away, but home has not yet become a dream. <u>This</u> is a dream, and home the only real reality I know.

Our Places of the Heart

Other than *love*, there may be no more important and universally meaningful word in the human language than *home*. Home is the place we create with our best intentions, so we and our family members have a safe, nurturing, loving environment to grow and

My father and the family he left behind in his hometown of Bensenville, Illinois.

thrive in. Few of us manage to create that perfect home we see in movies; however, we often come close enough to establish lasting ties that bind us and a sense of place that gives us a feeling of security and contentedness.

A happy home becomes a lighthouse for our ship when we travel to new horizons. No matter how long we are away and how happy we may be on our journey, home usually beckons us to return. Author Dennis Depcik reminds us of the importance of hearing back from those at home while away during his time in the army. Letters, he writes, are the "only link to the world that once was—our only link to those who love us, or who we hope at least care enough to see if we still exist. Mail proves there is a world out there—and maybe, just maybe, we're still a part of it."[32]

Home was an especially grounding memory, an essential ray of hope and reality for servicemen stationed at military bases or overseas in foreign wars. The army understood this well. In a letter to all parents whose sons found themselves at basic training camp in Camp Breckenridge in 1949, my father's captain wrote, "You must, of course, realize that the sudden change from the civilian to the military way of life is very often confusing to the young man just entering the army. Letters from friends and relatives are of great help to him at this time, especially if they are cheerful and express confidence in his success. May I count on you to assist him in this way?"

Today, emails work well to convey one's homesick feelings to those back home, yet something profound is missing when the recipient cannot touch or see the paper that tangibly holds those thoughts. Electronic messages give us little to hold on to—we cannot feel the paper that our loved ones held themselves or perhaps even kissed or cried over before sending them home. We can too easily lose the special flourishes, creativity, and soul of the writer when we convert our analog writing into digital communications. Thankfully,

there are still letter enthusiasts and volunteers who put pen to paper for military men and women, bringing joy to homesick souls.

As I read and transcribed my father's army letters into the computer, his messy, untamed handwriting was suddenly "prettified" on the screen. The color and emotion I had just felt in his handwritten words drained away. The translation from handwritten word to computer type stripped the soul from his words.

Handwritten letters give us more than information—they give us the essence of the person we so dearly miss. And this is perhaps why my grandmother could not bring herself to throw these letters away—even though her young son came home safely to her many decades earlier. My father's letters were the only thing in the world that had tied her to her "wandering boy" for two years. I can only imagine the sense of joy she felt upon reading his very last letter home.

Letters from a Stranger

Some days, it is hard to be human. I have always found it difficult to be an eyewitness to tragedy and loss and to the worst of who we are as human beings. Whenever there is a significant natural catastrophe, an environmental disaster, when war erupts, or there are senseless acts of gun violence, I must look away from the news for a time. Once I have had some time to process the news in smaller, more tolerable doses, I can decide if there might be a role for me in helping those who are suffering.

Like me, most people have a great amount of empathy for others going through difficult times. And while most of us do not have the power to stop wars, eliminate hunger, or prevent hurricanes, we can do something. Letter writing has a role to play in addressing human loss and suffering—even when it means writing letters to total strangers.

Imagine yourself, for example, having recently survived a natural disaster where you lost every possession you have ever owned, including your home. Picture yourself thirsty, dirty, hungry, and with only the clothes on your back. An aid agency provides you with a large box of emergency supplies to tide you over until you can secure permanent shelter. Wouldn't it be wonderful if also inside this box was a surprise: a short, caring letter from a stranger, someone who bears witness to all you have lost. This letter could serve as a bright light in the darkness for people in need. In a simple letter, you might just find the inspiration to keep moving ahead. For just a moment, you might find a sense of peace and connection.

Could Letters from a Stranger Also Reduce Loneliness?

In 2016, the Harris Poll conducted a survey of more than 2,000 Americans. The poll found that up to three-quarters (72 percent) of Americans experience loneliness. And for many, it is not just a once-in-a-while occurrence—one-third say they feel lonely at least once a week.[33]

These statistics merit serious attention by those of us who are fortunate enough to have meaningful connections in our lives. It is easy to see how people become isolated and disconnected from the larger community or even within their own families. This can lead to depression and a sense of hopelessness.

Research by Dr. Julianne Holt-Lunstad discovered that the epidemic of loneliness is more harmful to our health than smoking fifteen cigarettes a day and that there are few things in life with as large an impact on both the length and quality of our lives as the number of our social connections.[34]

Sometimes emotional hunger can be nearly as devastating to our health as physical hunger. Many people struggle emotionally each day, be it from natural disasters, broken families, bullying, addictions, mental illness, abuse, loneliness, or any number of other issues. When we find ourselves in the middle of an emotional struggle, it can feel as if we are the only ones in the world suffering that way. In those times, we do not want to feel alone or abandoned by others. We want confirmation that our plight, our specific situation, is of concern to someone, that there is a community that cares about our well-being.

Only within the past several years have I started reaching out to strangers in my community. It has been a rich experience, mostly for me and I hope for those I seek to support. We can each find a way to make a difference in the lives of total strangers, and the simple act of *writing letters* can be one of them.

Consider the impact these individuals had on the lives of total strangers, just by writing letters:

- A ninety-eight-year-old woman has handwritten more than seven thousand letters to service members overseas whom she has never met. Because her own son suffered from post-traumatic stress disorder due to his Vietnam War experience, she wanted to send simple offerings to others who may be far away from family and feel lonely or disconnected from the larger world.[35] Her sacrifice is small but her impact incalculable.
- A group of strangers diagnosed with bipolar disorder created a place to share their letters with each other, within their own chapter organization, and externally with others in the larger organization, the National Alliance on Mental Illness. One writer, Diana Chao, finds the exchange of letters nothing short of life-changing. She wisely observes that "writing is humanity distilled into ink."[36] By sharing her struggles with others, she no longer feels alone. She and others in the network who are struggling finally felt seen. "In a letter to a stranger," she says, "we forget the burden of judgment and fears. In the letters we read, we are no longer alone. Someone, somewhere thinks of us, too. We learn to care, to pay attention, to feel. In our growing empathy for others, we learn kindness, too, for ourselves."[37]
- Spurred by her own sense of loneliness and isolation while living in New York City after college, Hannah Brencher founded an organization called The World Needs More Love Letters in 2011. Her organization's purpose is to spread joy through random letters. The letters are left in subways, in library books, coffee shops, on park benches, and other public places and read by total strangers. Her letters are meant to brighten the recipient's day and offer encouragement and hope to whoever finds them.[38]

- An organization called Love for Our Elders asks volunteers to make cards for elderly people that the organization delivers to people in nursing homes and other care settings. A simple, handwritten card and greeting can mean the world to those who may feel alone and isolated in places removed from the hubbub of everyday living.
- A Saint Paul, Minnesota, woman decided one day to finally express her appreciation to neighbors who had planted a stunning flower garden in their yard. Each time she passed by it, she was impressed by its beauty. She did not know these neighbors, but she took a risk and wrote them a postcard expressing her gratitude for what they had done to beautify the neighborhood. Never expecting a response, she was delighted to find a card in her mailbox several weeks later. Her small effort apparently had given her gardening neighbors great joy, and they wanted her to know how much her kind words had meant to them.
- In response to the COVID-19 pandemic in 2020, the Oregon Humanities decided to bring people under stay-at-home orders together through the exchange of handwritten letters among total strangers.[39] This effort built upon previous work aimed at encouraging civic understanding through the exchange of handwritten letters. There was an immediate surge of interest in the letter-writing program while citizens were required to shelter in place. Ben Waterhouse, communications director at Oregon Humanities, found that the value of the letters was "in the connection" between people who found themselves in similar, difficult circumstances regardless of race, level of education, or their living circumstances.[40] Letter writers shared their deep feelings, fears, reflections, concerns, as well as wishes for good health. The letters were sent to strangers, even though the writers were not always certain that they would receive a letter in return. But responses to their letters often arrived quickly.

- Losing a mother to leukemia when she was ten years old inspired Grace Berbig to create an organization with the sole purpose of cheering up and providing emotional support for children suffering from cancer and other serious illnesses. Working with clubs in Minnesota, twelve other states, and six other countries, they craft handmade cards for seriously ill children and their families. Her nonprofit, Letters of Love, has delivered over one hundred thousand cards and notes for kids in hospital settings and treatment centers across the country and world.[41]

Doing a kind act for someone else helps us to feel better about ourselves and the world we live in. Whether it is for a stranger or someone you are closely connected to, a handwritten letter can make a significant difference in the lives of those in need. There is a world of need out there just waiting for our empathy and action.

The Sympathy Letter

If you have never lost someone you deeply loved, you might find it hard to imagine how much a handwritten sympathy card or letter can mean to those who are grieving. In fact, sympathy cards and letters matter a great deal more than you might ever realize. Every bit of effort you make to acknowledge the loss someone else has experienced helps them to heal and find a sense of purpose again. The time and the care you take in finding the right stationery or card, composing the right words, and offering comfort is truly soulful work.

While it is true that we all lead busy lives, it is best to avoid taking shortcuts when offering your sympathy. Texts and emails lack the personal touch so needed in times of loss. And it is never a good idea simply to sign your name on a commercial sympathy card and believe you have done your duty. Letters of condolence are not easy to write, but please do try to express your sympathy and caring on paper.

If possible, write your card or letter as soon after the death so that you are writing at a time when heartfelt emotions are still present and the shock has not yet worn off. Strive to write something with an authentic, spontaneous voice of sincerity. Visualize the person you are writing your condolences to, then let your heart speak.

Author Steven Petrow described his recent experience writing letters of sympathy during the COVID-19 pandemic: "Not because it's more 'proper' to handwrite a note than to use e-mail or post thoughts on social media, but because a death is so concrete and so permanent, so, too, should be the means of how we express our loss."[42]

Society expects us not to dwell on loss and to quickly "get over it." However, for most people, moving through grief is a long and difficult process that cannot be rushed. In a time of loss, it is so important for us to hear that our loved one's life mattered to others (over and over again), and that they, like you, understood and valued the unique gifts your loved one brought to the world. Even if the sentiments are not perfectly communicated, they still mean so much. When we feel that our community shares and supports us in our grief, we can better navigate the inevitable waves of emotion after a loss. Rejoining life becomes easier if our friends and relatives give us the support and space to grieve at our own pace.

It can take a long time to regain our footing and to make sense of our lives without the person we cherished. I have lost three members of my immediate family. Each death left me bereft and unmoored for a time. Probably the hardest loss was my brother, Lee, two years my senior, who died from brain cancer. He was taken from us in his prime, just as his life was blossoming and offering new and fulfilling opportunities.

Lee was a bright light in the world—sensitive, loving, incredibly witty, and endlessly giving. He was the life of the party and the center of our family. When he became ill and then died, I found it difficult to get through the days. I had two small children who needed me, and I found it hard to be fully present for them or to be completely focused on my career. I felt I couldn't talk about it freely without some people seeing me as "weak"—someone who just couldn't "get over it."

Receiving sympathy letters and cards was a lifeline that first year after Lee died. Each card or letter helped my family and me heal the open wounds of our grief. Because of my brother's charismatic personality, many of his colleagues and friends reached out to us to tell us funny, surprising, and touching stories about him. Each card and letter was a gift, a treasured memento of his life. Their letters helped us talk, relive, remember, and celebrate all that he brought to this world. The letters also allowed us to cry and laugh together, releasing pent-up emotions. We knew he was special, but the love and devotion of his friends and the great pains they took to share stories about him helped us along the path to living fully again.

In response to my survey about letter writing, one respondent states it well: "The handwritten letters I received after my mother died sustained me through that difficult time, especially those that shared their memories of her. It reminded me that she touched many lives beyond mine."

Providing comfort. Bearing witness. Reaching out. Sharing. Showing devotion and support. These are things letters help us to do so well if we only invest the time. If you are able, please take the time to show you care in writing and in person. Do not worry about perfection. The lives of the grieving are anything but perfect as they struggle to adapt to their new, harsh reality.

Consider writing a page or two to tell the grieving a story or two about their lost lover, family member, or friend. Let them know you are there for them and that you are willing and ready to talk about their loved one whenever they need to. Tell them that you care about them as they work through their grief and that it is okay to feel lost for a time. These words mean as much to the grieving as water does to someone lost at sea.

If you feel anxious about how to write a sympathy letter, consider visiting the many websites that offer good advice and helpful guidelines. These ideas are starting points, so please try not to create a sympathy letter that follows a boilerplate approach. Personalize it with your own stories and memories.

After sharing your initial sympathy letter or card, it can be helpful to those who are grieving to receive a follow-up letter or phone call. Once the funeral is over, when the visits, cards, and phone calls stop coming, this is often the most difficult time for those who have lost a loved one. The arrival of additional letters and cards can help the grieving begin their long healing journey.

Acknowledging someone's death is never easy. It is uncomfortable and sad. In these times, we can try to resist doing what is easier—sending an email or text—and instead make a little extra effort that will bring the greatest comfort. The death of a loved one is one of life's most challenging experiences for anyone. Our ability to soothe and support those who are grieving is immeasurably important, and assuredly unforgettable.

Letters That Hurt

The Poison Pen

Letters can be a tool for immeasurable good. But in the hands of a spiteful person, they can cause a path of destruction that is difficult to forget and impossible to erase.

Spoken words can fade with time, but hurtful letters written with the intent to inflict pain linger forever. The person writing the letter may feel quite smug, believing that their letter gives them the last word and the ability to cast the final judgment on someone else—whether it is through blaming, shaming, or denigrating. When the author wants to ratchet up the pain even more, they send their cruel letters anonymously. The truth, however, is that the person who is slinging the petty, hurtful, disparaging, threatening, or cruel words reveals more about their broken character than anything else.

In my mind, there is a distinct difference between a purposefully unkind poison pen letter and a letter that unintentionally causes hurt feelings by conveying a message that the recipient misinterprets or doesn't want to hear.

Sending a poison pen letter never ends well; in fact, it often causes permanent estrangement among people who, at one point, presumably cared for one another.

"I have received what I would describe as hate mail for my strong views and activism," one of my informal letters survey participants writes. "Those letters changed my life in that they made me more committed and strengthened my belief that I was on the right course."

During midlife, my grandfather and his sister became estranged over a stressful family situation. During their estrangement, his sister would regularly send him poison pen letters to further stoke anger and division. The letters were simply hurtful and unfair, he believed. After ten years of receiving her poison pen letters, his sister finally approached him at a family reunion and initiated a simple conversation. Because of my grandfather's forgiving nature, they were able to patch up their differences, though their relationship was never completely the same.

Should you ever feel tempted to write an angry letter, think twice, even thrice, before you send it. Sleep on the idea for a night or two before you begin writing—whether it is in an email or a paper letter. It might feel good to get those feelings out of your system at the time you are writing it, but letters can hang around in boxes and drawers for many years. What kind of legacy do you want to leave with your name signed to it?

Instead, take the high road with letter writing. Whenever possible, talk in person with the other party whom you feel has hurt you. It takes bravery to speak our truths face-to-face with someone, but if you decide to send a letter, it should always be civil and straightforward. If the letter is constructive, writing it can be cathartic for the author, provide clarity for the recipient, and potentially open the door to more communication between them.

In the best of circumstances, an honest letter might provide closure that allows two people to find common ground and help both move forward in a healthy manner. However, be prepared for the possibility that your tactful but truthful letter may backfire in an unintended way. Those of us who have tried to write a letter like this know that, without verbal cues and body language to accompany our words, misunderstandings can occur.

This is unfortunate, to be sure, but we shouldn't be afraid to communicate even if our words can sometimes be misconstrued. It seems important that we err on the side of communicating our feelings with honesty and openness. When we are trying to be open and constructive in expressing our confusion, it is probably better to experience the pain of working through conflict, which is inevitable in any relationship between two people, than never resolving a conflict at all. And the good news is those airing grievances constructively on paper or in person can sometimes initiate a reconciliation if both parties are ready to listen to one another. That is a goal worth pursuing.

If you have authored a poison pen letter in the past, consider writing a letter of apology to the recipient. It is never too late. The experience will be healing for you and, with luck, to the person you may have harmed.

Dear John/Jane Letters

The long-awaited love letter is finally in his hands. Using a small, red pocketknife, he opens the letter with great care and tosses the empty envelope onto his bunk bed. The anticipation rises as he slowly unfolds the sky-blue writing paper.

"Dear John," it begins. The next sentences are uncharacteristically formal and curt, the language too polite. Something is amiss. He feels it in his gut right away. He continues reading. The next sentences confirm his worst fears.

> John, I am finding it difficult to say this, but I have recently met someone new. He works at the same store as I do. He is a fine person and a real gentleman. We began dating several months ago, and our relationship has become quite serious. I think it best if you and I end our relationship now.
>
> I am grateful for the times we spent together, but I have always had the feeling that things would not work out between us. Please forgive me for having to make this

> decision. I am certain that you will find someone who deserves you more than I do. You have so much to offer.

He cannot believe what he has just read. It takes a moment to sink in. His tears begin to fall with an audible splash on the paper. Tiny pools gather, dissolving and blurring the ink. He releases a muffled moan. He wishes he could hide his pain, but this letter has cut him deeply.

Disbelief quickly turns to fury. His strong, long fingers slowly encircle the letter, then crush it into a ball. It falls onto the floor and rolls under his bunk. He doesn't care. The woman he loved and dreamed about, his fiancée for more than a year, the woman he believed loved him in return, has betrayed him. There are no words that adequately describe his devastation.

His sense of defeat and loneliness is crushing. He can hardly breathe. Some of his military buddies can sense what is going on. Several of them have received similar messages, all cruelly ending long-distance relationships and crushing their accompanying hopes and dreams. They are watching John closely now to ensure that he does not do anything drastic as has been the case with other soldiers before. They understand that losing the one good thing that was their link to the beauty and normalcy of home can mean losing hope.

Before electronic forms of communication were commonplace, timid lovers used this style of brush-off to end a deeply personal connection. It was especially painful when a third party was involved, when the severing of ties was completely unexpected, or if a letter was written in an insensitive way that put a quick and complete ending to a close relationship.

Receiving a letter of this kind was a familiar enough experience that people adopted a specific name for it. Most of us are still familiar with the term *Dear John* or *Dear Jane* letter.

Origins

The origin of the "Dear John" letter is believed to date back to the 1862 poem "No, Thank You, John" by the Victorian poet Christina Rossetti. Later, a female protagonist named Alice Vavasor, in Anthony Trollope's 1864 novel *Can You Forgive Her?* uses it in an "end of our affair" letter to her lover, John Grey. She begins the letter with "Dear John."[43]

A popular music-hall song from the early 1900s also included the words

Dear John, I love you so
Dear John, you've got to go
Dear John, I love you so
Dear John, you must go.[44]

Perhaps the strongest influence that led to coining the term *Dear John letter* was during the World War II era, when many men spent years overseas, away from their girlfriends, fiancées, or wives. Their lovers, thousands of miles away back home, sometimes strayed with other men. After finding new love, wives and girlfriends would commonly write letters to their soldiers overseas, giving them the dreaded news: the relationship was over. Among the jilted lovers in the military, these letters would become known as "Dear Johns."[45]

Since then, the term *Dear John letter* has been used more broadly to describe any letter written by a woman that ends a once-close relationship and does the hurtful deed without seeing their ex-lover again. Similarly, Dear Jane letters are written by men wishing to end a relationship with a lover without having to confront her face-to-face.

Dear John/Jane letters can run the gamut of emotions, from a soft ending to an affair to no attempt to protect sensitive feelings. It is never easy to get the brush-off, even when it is done with kindness and sensitivity. I know. Many years ago, I was the recipient of a Dear Jane letter myself.

During graduate school, I dated a sweet, caring man who seemed to take a serious interest in me. We seemed to have a great deal in common and got along very well. Not surprisingly, I fell head over heels for him. I was a midwesterner; he an East Coast man. We met at a tumultuous time in our lives when we were both working hard to carve out our own career paths. I was certain that we could find a way to do this together. He apparently did not. He returned to the East Coast with the promise of taking the time to figure things out. I waited, hoping that he would reconsider and see that we needed to be together.

As I began my second year of graduate school, he continued to call and write me. There were mixed signals. I finally wrote, asking him to clarify his intention for our relationship, given that other men had begun asking me out and I was not sure whether I should accept their invitations.

Not long after that, the day arrived when I found a letter from him in my mailbox. I remember the anticipation and the dread. Would my heart be crushed? Would he surprise me? I began to read his four-page letter. The letter was kind and reflective. He wrote some lovely things about our time together; however, there were things he detailed in the letter that felt like a sucker punch. They stuck out on the page as if in neon lights:

- We had a great deal in common, but he didn't have the peace of mind to make a commitment to me.
- We were simply not right for one another when it came to marriage.
- I had a lot to offer someone, but he wouldn't want to hold me back "if I found someone more receptive out there."

The finality of that last sentence made it clear. It was over. I felt gutted and betrayed. I found myself unable to concentrate on my studies. I spent a lot of time in my apartment staring at the corner of the ceiling by my front door. A few other letters went back and forth between us that helped me understand his motives and feelings, but our breakup remained a painful experience for me.

Then something unexpected happened.

About a week after I exchanged my last letter with him, a quiet, handsome man who was in my environmental policy class called me unexpectedly one night and asked me to go to a movie. I agreed, not from a place of enthusiasm but from the inability to say no to someone who seemed very smart, gentle, and earnest.

Our first date was pleasant enough, but my mind was elsewhere. However, over the following weeks, he kept calling me and bringing me small, romantic gifts. He also seemed to appreciate our time together and to take the relationship seriously. Within six months, we were sure we wanted to be committed to one another, and this time, it stuck. The Dear Jane letter from my past lover no longer seemed terribly important to me. And now, more than thirty-five years later, I see that one ending led to the possibility of something better happening to me—meeting and later marrying my husband.

For most of us, receiving a Dear John or Jane letter can surely be painful, but in an odd way, we may have gotten a gift in disguise. Sometime in the future, we may want to thank our old lovers for seeing what might not have been obvious to us at the time. We should, perhaps, have been more grateful to them for saving us from additional pain and for setting us free. I now see that my Dear Jane letter was a badge of honor. I took a risk by being in a relationship and allowing myself to fall in love. The lover turned out not to be the great match that I'd hoped. No mind. I am glad I was willing to take that risk. At the end of the affair, I found myself still standing and much wiser and more able to recognize real love when it came along.

These days, Dear John and Jane letters have turned into text messages, the ultimate in cruelty because of their brevity. In some cases, there may not even be the crumb of communication offered when severing these ties. Ex-lovers are simply ghosted instead.

Receiving a handwritten letter of explanation is painful and hard enough to decipher and understand. But sending no message at all is deeply offensive, showing little empathy or regard for the ex-lover. Neither party gains understanding. Neither party gets closure.

An old-fashioned, three-dimensional, handwritten brush-off letter not only brings closure but also has the added value of providing the jilted lover with a tangible memento of love lost or wisdom gained. A respondent to my informal letters survey shared with me a twist on a Dear Jane letter. While she had not directly received a brush-off letter from her lover, she found one that had the same effect. She tells it this way:

"I found a handwritten letter my husband wrote to his lover. It was a rough draft tucked under the bed. He wrote it out nice, I was told, before he sent it. This letter devastated me. We had a six-month-old son. It took thirteen years to leave him, but I did. It was hell. And I kept the letter."

I kept my Dear Jane letter, too, because it represents an important time in my life and my own development. The year my boyfriend and I were together was a happy one, and I don't believe it is ever wrong to love someone—even if they cannot love you back the same way.

For others, keeping a Dear Jane letter would simply be impossible—a constant memento of a love affair gone wrong. For some, a Dear John/Jane letter might instead become the kindling for a celebratory fire commemorating the end of the affair. With the strike of a match, the scorned lover can forever release what no longer serves them as the letter becomes smoke and ash. Letters can also be shredded, crumpled, stomped on. If you receive a Dear Jane letter and it especially stings, I encourage you to get creative with its destruction if need be!

Sadly, deleting text messages just doesn't seem to offer today's rejected lover the same delicious opportunities for getting mad and getting even. Here again, the handwritten letter is simply irreplaceable.

Letters That Heal

According to psychologists and researchers, expressing our innermost thoughts and deepest emotions in writing can have considerable mental and physical health benefits. In fact, research finds that individuals who agreed to write about traumatic, stressful, or emotional life events for just fifteen to twenty minutes on three to five occasions have significantly better physical and psychological outcomes compared with those who wrote about more neutral topics.[46]

Because of its many benefits, some mental health practitioners encourage their clients to use "expressive" or "therapeutic" writing as part of their therapy. Expressive writing allows them to explore personal feelings and experiences in an authentic and unfiltered way. Expressive writing is rarely shown to anyone else, so clients can write freely and without judgment.

Expressive writing for short periods of time has been shown to promote improved interpersonal interactions and memory, as well as feelings of well-being. There were more pronounced short-term and longer-term improvements, however, when it came to its impacts on physical well-being, including improved blood pressure, lung function, and immune system functioning.[47]

University of Texas social psychologist Dr. James Pennebaker has long been a pioneer of writing therapy. His groundbreaking work has influenced numerous additional research studies in this area and been effective in helping thousands of patients explore and reevaluate their own sources of anxiety, unsettling thoughts, grief, and trauma.

With writing clinician and integrative health coach Dr. John Evans, Pennebaker coauthored a book on this subject, *Expressive Writing: Words That Heal*. In their book, Pennebaker and Evans explore the ways expressive writing can help patients become more compassionate with themselves and others, ask for or confer their forgiveness about a challenging life event, and voice empathy or gratitude for the people in their lives.[48]

Letter writing can be a powerful form of expression. Pennebaker and Evans have found that clients who write a specific "transactional" letter often find that it has great therapeutic value in learning how to unpack and cope with deep emotional traumas. Transactional writing "gets you beyond what you thought you could not get over," Evans says.

Professionals typically use transactional letters to conduct day-to-day business in a variety of fields. They are used to convey something of importance between two people, to meet certain agreed-upon expectations, to address a particular obligation someone has made to another. However, in mental health settings, a person uses a transactional letter to take care of the business of their emotional life.[49]

Patients write transactional letters with a specific individual in mind. They might have a close relationship with the individual they are writing to, or conversely, the recipient may be a total stranger who happened to play an important role in their lives. Sometimes, a patient writes a letter to themselves. The value in writing a letter comes from having to slow down, carefully consider thoughts and feelings, and then organize them clearly on paper.[50]

Pennebaker and Evans encourage patients to use a typical letter format, following some of the basic letter-writing conventions with respect to structure, grammar, punctuation, and the like. At the same time, the writer should not worry too much about perfection when expressing themselves. Pennebaker and Evans encourage patients to express their thoughts, feelings, opinions, and judgments about a particular situation or event as clearly and constructively as possible. It may take several drafts of the letter to accomplish this goal.[51]

Therapists find that when patients write letters as a part of their therapy, the experience serves to enhance the progress they are making in one-on-one counseling sessions. Letters help individuals step back, gain perspective, and work through an unaddressed trauma or incident.[52] The writing exercise is less about sending the letter than it is about the process of unpacking and coming to terms with feelings and thoughts a client may have never come to terms with. Pennebaker and Evans advise that, in many cases, it may be best never to send the letter at all.[53] A licensed psychologist can advise you on the best course of action.

Handwritten Letters Provide Many Paths to Healing

Because many of us are not able to understand our deepest struggles or verbally express our feelings, Pennebaker and Evans offer several options for doing so with the written word. Depending on the experiences, circumstances, and their clients' needs, they offer five different kinds of letters that can be written to explore and come to terms with what has happened to them. Writing the letter is an important and positive step in healing and unburdening the pain and obsessive thinking that often accompany trauma. The five types of letters are:[54]

- **The Compassionate Letter.** Written if you yourself have experienced trauma and wish to offer advice to someone else currently going through a similar situation.

- **The Empathetic Letter.** Written for yourself or someone else involved in a disturbing event, whereby you endeavor to understand your own motives or actions—or theirs.
- **The Gratitude Letter.** Written to those in your life who have given you something important, done something for you, taught you, or inspired you.
- **The Granting Forgiveness Letter.** Written for those you need to forgive for something they did, said, or did not do or say.
- **The Asking Forgiveness Letter.** Written to someone you may have harmed with your words or deeds, for expressing one's apology, and for requesting their forgiveness.

For more information about writing these letters, consult Pennebaker and Evans's book or a qualified mental health provider.

Who among us has not had reason to benefit from writing or receiving the kinds of transactional letters described by Pennebaker and Evans at some point in our lives? Letters matter. Letters can heal.

Let's explore two vastly different, unrelated stories about the way letters helped to heal broken hearts. In one case, the letter writer caused the most grievous harm possible to others. The other incident involved a much less significant act of cruelty.

Letters That Healed in the Darkest of Places

"I was a young drug dealer with a quick temper and a semiautomatic pistol," admits Shaka Senghor, an ex-convict, now an accomplished author and speaker. At the age of nineteen, Senghor, who grew up in a disadvantaged household in Detroit, killed a man in cold blood during a drug deal that went terribly wrong. Arrested and tried for that crime, he would serve nineteen years in prison.

During the early years of his incarceration, he became increasingly bitter and angry, and soon found himself involved in illegal activities inside the prison, including more drug dealing. His illegal actions landed him in solitary confinement for seven years, where he struggled to endure what he calls the "darkest possible place."[55]

During his time in solitary confinement, he received numerous life-changing letters. The first came from his young son, who sparked the beginning of his long journey of acknowledgment, apology, and atonement for his crimes. Another critically important letter came from his victim's family. In it, they offered Senghor their forgiveness for killing their son. Senghor's father also wrote to him regularly, assuring him that he would never leave his side.[56]

Letters became a lifeline over Senghor's long imprisonment, keeping him strong and focused on his path to redemption and rehabilitation.

> My transformation really started with letters from my dad. He is a beautiful letter writer, and he would write me five- to six-page handwritten letters about life. We did a lot of healing and growing together through our letters.
>
> And in my toughest moments in prison, I would go back and reread his letters as a reminder that there was someone on the other side of the four walls who really cared about me . . . Through our letters we were able to be really honest and very transparent with each other . . . I felt like the intimacy of the letters between my dad and I were something we just don't see: an honest and emotional exchange between Black men.[57]

Now a successful author, Senghor has recently written his second book, a collection of letters for his own sons, entitled *Letters to the Sons of Society*. The book focuses on the power of love and its ability to liberate our lives. "Love is truly our power and is the source of all things great . . . My responsibility is to empower my sons with my truth," he says.

A Letter, Asking Forgiveness, Arrives Many Years After the Fact

We sat in the cozy family room of my friend's home one day, drinking wine and sharing our latest triumphs and struggles. My friend sat back in her tan lounge chair, glass of wine in hand. Suddenly, she stood, saying, "I want to show you something!" She went over to her desk and looked intently at a small envelope. "Remember years ago when I told you about the toxic writers' group I was in, the one where a woman told me that I wasn't a good fit and I should leave the group? She had coldly explained to me that my writing critiques lacked depth, which was deeply hurtful. I'd given what I considered to be thoughtful comments on each member's writings, both on paper and in our meetings—comments I hoped would be helpful."

"Yes," I said. "I remember that. It sounded mean-spirited of her and unfair."

"Well," she continued, "I haven't seen or spoken to anyone from that group for years. Now, out of the blue, I received a card from the person who told me I had to leave the group. I couldn't believe it, after all these years! Why would she of all people be writing now?"

My friend sat back in her chair again, opened the envelope, and began reading the message to me from a pretty blue-and-white note card. The writer's message had a warm, conciliatory, highly apologetic message. The writer did not try to make excuses for her behaviors. Instead, she asked for my friend's forgiveness for the "shabby way" she had treated her. She also acknowledged that my friend's expulsion from the writers' group had resulted in the breakup of the group, as well as some long-standing friendships.

It was clear from the tone and content of the letter that this woman was trying to make amends for the wounds she had caused. We understood the courage and self-awareness it took to write that letter. We wondered about the timing of this note and what might have propelled her to contact my friend after so many years. Was it the COVID-19 pandemic that left her wanting to address her unresolved regrets?

We may never know.

My friend became quiet for a moment. Then she said, "One thing I keep learning as I get older is that no one is *just one thing*. I've known this my whole life, but new examples keep surfacing."

"Yes," I said, "we all are so incredibly complex. Not all good, not all bad."

As I prepared to leave, my friend told me that she might acknowledge the note somehow. "I deleted her email long ago," she said. "But there is an address on the card . . ."

"That's a great idea," I said. "It took a lot of guts to write that note, and it would be nice to acknowledge that you appreciated the gesture."

Writing expressively, whether to communicate empathy or appreciation, to ask for forgiveness, to provide support, or to vent our frustrations on paper for our own benefit alone are all deeply soulful acts—soothing and restorative. We can find redemption and transformation when we dig deep and offer the best of ourselves to those people with whom we have troubled relationships. Here, we can begin the process of writing ourselves well, bring wholeness to our lives, and needed healing to those who have mattered to us.

Pen Pal Letters: A Whole New World Awaits

The idea of being a pen pal with a stranger first became popular in the early 1900s. Pen pals were initially called "pen friends." The term *pen friend* first appeared in the *Oxford Dictionary* in 1919. Pen friends were described as someone who corresponded with people over vast differences and distances. For more than a century, people have been seeking pen pals because of a desire to learn about different cultures, languages, and countries.[58]

Childhood Pen Pals

I had the good fortune of growing up in an excellent school district in Illinois. As early as the 1960s, it offered students an opportunity to learn a foreign language, beginning in the third grade. At that time, the only language offered to us was French.

Our early years of French instruction focused on building vocabulary and practicing pronunciation. Ms. Erickson was my first French instructor, and she would continue to be through eighth grade. She had studied French in Paris, which at the time seemed quite adventurous for a single woman to do. Most Americans did not travel much back then, so her firsthand experience in France made an impression on me.

In eighth grade, Ms. Erickson gave us an exciting new opportunity: the chance to be pen pals with French students who were our ages. I jumped at the chance. I learned that my pen pal's name was Brigitte and she lived in Marzy, in the French region of Bourgogne. Writing to her for the first time was daunting. I knew I had better keep the letter short and simple because I was not yet very fluent in this new language, and I remember struggling a great deal to write it. Anticipation grew as I awaited her response.

Receiving Brigitte's first sky-blue aerogram was a thrill I still remember all these years later. Each time another one arrived, I dropped everything I was doing, gleefully sliced open the trifold envelope, quickly located my French-English dictionary, and painstakingly translated her words as I read. Sometimes she included pictures with her letters, and I was given a small glimpse into her day-to-day life in the French countryside.

Brigitte and I continued writing back and forth over a period of four or five years. I learned about her school, the town she lived in, her family life, her pets, interests. We wrote mostly about the simple things we liked to do outside of school, where we had gone on vacation, and so on. She seemed studious and curious like I was, and our friendship grew over time, though I would not characterize it as a close relationship. The language barrier made it difficult—for me at least—to write about the more personal things I was going through.

The year I stopped taking French classes and became more focused on college and other pursuits, I stopped writing to Brigitte. I stopped writing mostly out of fear that I would not be able to keep up with her level of fluency. I have regretted that many times since but have never forgotten her.

Over those years of exchanging letters, I learned something valuable about French life and culture. I also discovered that she and I, living thousands of miles apart and coming from very different cultures, had a good deal in common. Because of her letters, I began to think of myself not only as a citizen of the United States but a global citizen as well. It was then that I decided I wanted to see the world and know more of its people. I had been bitten by a case of wanderlust I have never really gotten over.

Toward the end of the time when we were writing to one another, we exchanged Christmas gifts. Neither of us had a lot of money to spend, so her generosity meant a great deal to me. One Christmas, she sent me a beautiful etched-glass figurine of a mother bear and her cub. It sits on my bedroom dresser today. Often, when I look at it, I smile as I think about her generosity and thoughtfulness. The most amazing thing is that after nearly fifty years, I remember her letters and continue to remember *her*, regardless of the time that has passed and how much our world has changed since we were teenagers.

I still enjoy the charming glass bears given to me by my French pen pal decades ago.

If you have children and they have the chance to be part of a supervised program that connects them with a young pen pal in another country, please encourage them to participate! Having a pen pal will stimulate their curiosity about a special place in the world and perhaps increase their knowledge about new cultures and societies. Most importantly, it might open their hearts to getting to know people who are different from them. If they are fortunate, they might even make a friend for life.

Adult Pen Pals

In graduate school, I had a remarkable professor, Dr. Randall Baker, who taught international environmental management at Indiana University. Toward the end of my time there, we occasionally had lunch and became better acquainted. When I left Bloomington shortly after graduating, we began writing letters to each other. To my delight and surprise, it evolved into a thirty-five-year letter-writing odyssey. What made Randall such an interesting and enchanting writing companion was that he lived and worked all around the world, had an unusual and varied career, and was a prolific and beautiful writer. He also had one of the best and cleverest senses of humor I have ever known. I never imagined that our friendship would last so long. I owe this to the power of letter writing.

Over those years, I saw Randall in person on only a few occasions; however, his letters arrived with some regularity, originating from different countries and continents. He was among the first I knew who used a fountain pen, who created his own personalized stationery, and added clever and amusing embellishments and beautiful old stamps to the envelopes. His letters were always a feast for the eyes.

Randall was, without doubt, the person I exchanged the most letters with over the years. We often said that we were undoubtedly the last two people on the planet still writing letters on a regular basis. But what a gift and delight that regular correspondence was. We could have easily thrown down the paper and pen and started emailing each other, taking the path of least resistance. But thankfully, we continued in our familiar ways. I grieve deeply for my good friend, now gone, and for the end of our rewarding correspondence.

The Invisible Threads That Connect Us

Something powerful and beautiful emerges when a relationship stands the test of time. Sharing life experiences and our deepest feelings with others over and over creates trust and intimacy that can thrive over the long haul. As time goes on, each person becomes increasingly grateful for the predictability and security of that relationship. Long-term friendships like these have been profoundly important to me over my lifetime.

Maintaining long-distance friendships has not always been easy, though letter writing gives you a fighting chance to keep the relationship viable. Through the middle decades of my life, I confess that my letters arrived sporadically, were often on the brief side, and were more practical than prosaic. Somehow, despite changing jobs, child-rearing, and aging parents, my friends and I managed to track the major events, trials, and triumphs in each other's lives over a very long time. Some years, the annual Christmas letter had to suffice, and it was the only thing that connected us over several decades.

In recent years, once my family and work responsibilities waned, I decided to make it a priority to reconnect with several of my pen pals in person. I had not set eyes on two of these pen pals for about thirty years, so I wondered if we would recognize each other after all that time apart. Of course, we both physically had changed somewhat over the years. Yet what amazed me was how quickly and seamlessly we were able to reconnect on an emotional level again, as if no time had passed. Conversation was effortless and lively, the stories and experiences shared openly and warmly.

What these reunions taught me was how powerful those infrequent but reliable letters and cards had been in keeping our friendships intact for all those years. The initial instincts and intuition that once drew us together as friends in our younger years were as authentic and "right" today as they were decades before. Now that we have seen each other again face-to-face, it will be even easier to continue our friendship in a seamless way going forward—perhaps, if we are lucky, for another thirty years.

One of my old friends from Chicago whom I recently reconnected with in person stated it well in a recent Christmas card to me: "It was great seeing you this past year—and it was a joy to feel so comfortable with you, as if we were always seeing each other through life. The memories of our brief summer at the Lake Michigan Federation are very faded, however, a letter to each other every year was our connection throughout our lives."

Yes, we could have simply sent each other messages on email and Facebook for the past decades, but the old-fashioned discipline of letter writing offered what to us seemed to be a more personal, intimate, and meaningful connection that has stood the test of time. Perhaps seeing her handwriting on paper, her annual choice of Christmas card, and the photographs she occasionally tucked inside her cards enabled a stronger bond between us. As a result, we have been able to sustain a closeness that I am not certain we could have maintained in the same way using popular social media platforms.

Any respectful communication between people is good, whatever methods or tools. However, letters seem to build trust over time, across the miles, and through the perturbations of life. I feel such gratitude for the diligence and commitment of the friends I've had who were willing to keep this unique form of communication going. Had we given up or taken the easy way out, we would have surely lost something special in the process—a lasting, delightful, and rewarding friendship that has simply never failed us.

The Round Robin: The Letter That Keeps on Giving

Social media friend groups have their place in keeping people connected today, but before the internet, some groups of friends participated in a different kind of social network called a *round robin letter*. The letter I speak of here should not be confused with the round robin letter that creates feelings of dread among the citizens in the United Kingdom each year.[59] There, the round robin letter is what Americans would call the annual braggadocio Christmas letter. Nor is the round robin a chain letter that frightens people into participating or falsely promises them riches if they do.

Here in the United States, the concept of a round robin letter will probably get you a much more favorable reaction. The US-based letter is a hands-on, purely congenial way to ensure that a group of relatives or friends stay in touch and up to date with each other's thoughts, experiences, and significant life events in an intimate and meaningful way. To participate, one must employ real paper, pen, ink, and . . . the postal service, or so-called snail mail.

Think of the round robin as a snowball. It starts with one letter, and as it passes from house to house and hand to hand, it becomes something bigger and more robust over time. The round robin letter becomes a growing testament to the relentless passage of time and bears witness to the inevitable ups and downs of the lives of its contributors.

This is how it works:

A group of people determines that they want to stay in touch through handwritten letters. One member makes a list of people who want to participate. Someone in the group gets the process started by writing the initial round robin letter. The letter shares personal news and anything else that person feels like sharing with the rest of the group, such as cartoons, photos, or art to enhance the impact of the handwritten word. The letter is signed, sealed in an envelope, and sent off to the next person on the list.

Once the second person on the list reads the first letter, they write their own, then include the first letter along with theirs in a larger envelope and address it to the next person on the list. The post office does its duty and delivers the letters to the next person, who does precisely the same thing as those before, and so on.

Once everyone in your group has had the letter packet sent to them once, the circular letter writing practice begins again. When the packet lands back in the hands of the person who initiated the process, that person must remove their old letter and add a new one, keeping all other letters along with it, thus beginning the round robin process all over again. This ever-evolving circle of words continues for as long as everyone in the group remains committed to it.

It is best if your group is not too large, lest it take many months to have the packet of letters returned to you. When signing up for this group, the members must promise not to procrastinate too much when it is their time to write their own letter. Some groups request that each member take no more than two weeks to respond. Some round robin groups will go so far as to kick someone out of the group if they take too long to respond.

A dear friend of mine, Judy, first told me about the sweet round robin letter idea. A group of her friends at Mount Holyoke College in Massachusetts started one in the 1950s when it came time for all of them to go their separate ways. Her group's round robin went on for a year or two, she recalled. Yes, there were those pesky life events or someone's procrastination that would sometimes slow down their rotation, but overall, it was, she said, a delightful way to stay in touch with each other in a personal, interactive, and consistent way.

Round robin letters were not uncommon among college women who, once graduated, wanted to stay in touch. One such group of women friends from Oberlin College started their round robin letter group in 1951, and it continued for more than fifty years. The women preferred to continue with snail mail instead of converting to email, even though most members in the group used it regularly. "Email certainly has its place, but there is nothing like a good old-fashioned letter," says one member. "It's a dying art, but it is a great way to communicate. It's wonderful to hold a letter in your hand, read it, and reread it another day."[60]

In Nebraska, the Benson family had four sisters, a mother, and sister-in-law all participating in writing a round robin letter for more than fifty years as well. All members felt that this form of communication was essential to holding them together when distances threatened to pull them apart. As the sisters age, the younger generation of cousins have fought to keep the tradition going. The letters were one important way to keep cherished memories and family history alive.[61]

A daughter of one of the Benson sisters, Roxane Nelson, now has taken her mother's place among the round robin group. Reflecting on this long-standing family practice, Nelson comments, "I think it's important that we take time for the things that we love . . . people don't take time anymore for the people that they love."[62]

The Legacy Letter

If my father said it once, he said it a thousand times: "That will definitely be a chapter in my book." He would say this after reminiscing about a specific time in his life or after telling an entertaining story. In his later years, my father toyed with the idea of writing about his life experiences, but because he was a very modest man, he never did write that book. Like so many of us, he believed that no one would care about his "unremarkable" middle-class life. The reality is, he had quite an interesting life and was an engaging writer, and I am deeply saddened by the fact that we do not have his stories set down on paper for posterity.

People love a good story—any kind of story if told with clarity and honesty. We are wired to hear them, as they have helped to bind us in families and groups for many thousands of years. The stories we tell don't need to be about someone famous, heroic, exceptional, or fascinating, though sometimes they are. Nor do the stories have to have great historical or cultural value. We appreciate even the simplest of stories if they are relatable in some way or if they touch our hearts. That is why all our stories are important.

The stories of our elders can help us to navigate our own lives. In some cases, they help us create a better blueprint for living or avoid unnecessary pain and suffering. As time passes and we become more circumspect about our own lives, we also might feel the need to share or document our own experiences and the wisdom we've gained because of our own school of hard knocks.

We can choose to pass life lessons on to our children through oral tradition or by capturing stories using the written word. Legacy letters are one approach to sharing important life lessons with the friends and family members who outlive us.

What Is a Legacy Letter?

Johann Wolfgang von Goethe once said that "letters are the most significant memorial a person can leave." The idea of the legacy letter (sometimes called an *ethical will*) comes from an ancient Jewish tradition dating back to biblical times, around 1500 BCE.[63] On his deathbed, Jacob gathered his twelve sons to offer them his blessings, moral directives, and burial instructions upon his death. Rather than write it, Jacob verbally expressed his ethical will to each of his sons.[64]

Today, legacy letters are succinct documents written by anyone of any faith tradition. They are intended to be read by friends and family members when we die. Legacy letters are nonlegal, nonbinding documents that convey a person's values, experiences, and beliefs. Legacy letters can be very valuable, as they sometimes provide more important information than legal documents like a will or trust can.[65]

Legacy letters summarize what we want others to know or understand about who we were and what mattered to us. These letters often express values about wealth or our hopes for the future, convey our blessings, explain family secrets, voice regrets, give forgiveness, send healing thoughts, and more. In the process of writing a legacy letter, we can be quite succinct or communicate with greater depth and honesty. How you write a legacy letter is a personal decision, and there is no right or wrong way to write one.

Legacy letters help to ensure that nothing important that you want to say to someone remains unsaid. In this soulful, spiritual process, you can express yourself without superficial sentiments or the fear of judgment. Legacy letters are living documents, always open to revision or addendum over time.

In these busy times, it seems that families are sharing less about family history through storytelling. Having come from a family that regularly shared photographs and stories about previous generations, I am sometimes surprised by the number of people who have no idea who their ancestors were, what they did for a living, what they cared about or experienced in their lifetimes. Given this reality, legacy letters seem more important than ever.

We owe it to the ancestors who came before us to know something about the lives they led and the ways in which their experiences, sacrifices, and struggles may have influenced who we've become today, for better or worse. And perhaps we owe it to future generations to know enough about us so that they can put their own lives into a familial and historical context.

Legacy letters are a powerful tool that can weave our separate stories together into a meaningful and enlightening legacy for current and future generations.

Writing the Legacy Letter

Rachel Freed, author of *Your Legacy Matters: Harvesting the Love and Lessons of Your Life*, suggests using a simple format for writing your letter. She recommends keeping letters on the short side—even as little as one page, using one paragraph for each part.[66] Freed suggests writing for fifteen to thirty minutes at a time. As you write your legacy letter, you are not seeking perfection, only a draft of initial ideas. By limiting the amount of time you spend writing your letter, you are less likely to see it as a monumental task that feels like a burden and put it off. Do not allow "perfect" to get in the way of "good."

Freed suggests first selecting the people to whom you would like to send this letter. These important letters are usually written for family members, colleagues, friends, or a group of people who are important to you at any age. Reflect on the things you most want your loved ones to know about you or how you feel. Next, Freed recommends these four major steps to guide your work:[67]

- **Provide Context.** This portion provides a brief family history and denotes the date the letter was written to provide context for the reader. Was it written in your forties or your nineties?
- **Tell Your Story or Experience.** Use this portion of the letter to describe the highlights of your life that you most want to share. Tell about each experience in your own words.
- **Share Your Life Lessons from Your Story or Experiences.** This section shares the essence of who you are. Describe and discuss the most important values and lessons that came out of your life experiences.
- **Share a Blessing.** This is the core of a legacy letter. This part should flow from the previous parts. Here, you will want to share your feelings of love, appreciation, caring, and devotion

> for the people to whom you are writing. Imagine that this will be the final chance you have to tell them how important they are to you. It is important to keep criticisms and judgments out of your letters and avoid anything manipulative or hurtful.

Debbie Mycroft, who specializes in helping people write legacy letters, advises that once you have written your letter, show it to a trusted relative or friend. They can help you clarify messages or identify missing pieces of your story.[68] You can either immediately send the letter to its recipient, or it can be filed among your important papers to be delivered after your death. Be sure to enclose the letter in an addressed envelope so that your executor knows exactly who it is intended for.[69]

The beauty of the legacy letter is that it can be so many different things. It can be very serious, humorous, tender, revealing, or simply explanatory. Here's an example of a short legacy letter recently written by my husband, Allen Dotson, for our son, Ian:

> Dear Ian,
>
> August 2022
>
> On the eve of your twenty-second birthday, I wanted to tell you a bit about my childhood—something you may find mildly interesting someday, as you reflect more upon your own.
>
> You may recall that my paternal grandparents had a small farm about twenty miles northwest of Indianapolis. For my father, this farm was often a place of toil, hardships, and some unhappiness. For me, it was largely a source of salvation from the stressful environment I experienced at home. The farm was where I felt the greatest joys as a young child. While my grandparents and parents had problems in their

own lives, I was blissfully ignorant of them then. I still loved my grandparents and their farm and everything about it. I could wander their property freely, climb fences, visit the animals and help care for them, just be myself, and be, well … happy—purely happy.

Do you ever remember having an intense feeling of joy or excitement as a child when something you loved was about to happen? I hope that you do—that you were able to experience that type of happiness. That was the feeling I had on the days when my parents told me, before leaving for work, that we would be going to the farm that night—especially if it was a Friday night, and I thought I might be staying there for an entire weekend. I was as happy as I was on the last day of school each year—when freedom was at hand, and the possibilities seemed endless.

This small farm had an oversized influence on who I became—particularly, it developed my love of nature and all living things. Back then, there was a large garden, cows, a few horses, hundreds of chickens, hunting dogs, and barn cats. And then there were the wild creatures—raccoons, skunks, woodchucks, rabbits, owls, quail, red-tailed hawks, and crows. I would often converse with the quail and the crow, learning to imitate their calls quite accurately, and calling back and forth with them. I guess my enjoyment of talking with those birds should have told me that I would never really be happy in an office job.

I talked with the trees in the woods, too. You see, your father has been odd even longer than you thought. My "special tree" was a massive black oak, but there were also conversations with a large red oak and with a sycamore—a wonderful tree that doesn't grow here in the north. I buried a small treasure at the foot of the sycamore at about the time I was reading the book *Treasure Island*.

Another fond memory is of the lightning bug nights. In those days, there were fence rows where lightning bugs were plentiful. On hot summer evenings, my grandmother would give me a clean peanut butter jar with air holes punched in the lid, which she made with an old ice pick. After catching a jar full of bugs, I would watch them in the dark next to my bed until I fell asleep. In the morning, I was sad to find most of them dead, but I would repeat this act many times until one day when I was told I was too old to catch lightning bugs. But are you ever too old to catch lightning bugs? That's something to think about. I may be nearing the age when it's time to begin again.

There's a huge house on the farm now, and many more on neighboring farms. And I can't bear to know what has happened to the old oaks and sycamore trees. Some were more than two hundred years old, and the black oak was much older still. The people living there now want different things. They'll never know what that place and those creatures meant to me or others before me. I hope you, dear son, will always stay close to nature, have your special places, and experience the same kinds of joy that the old farm gave to me.

With love, Dad

Why Are Legacy Letters Important?

Because you are. Not long ago, I took a memoir-writing class in Minneapolis. The class was created for people aged fifty-five and older who wanted to explore their own stories through writing. Our group had six members, each of us from completely different life experiences. I suppose you could say that the class was comprised of "ordinary" Americans.

Our leader provided short writing prompts to get us started, and we then had fifteen minutes to write our stories. With each exercise, we wrote about a variety of subjects, over a period of several months. We wrote with abandon, not worrying much about perfection and having no time to edit our work. The things we wrote about were simple life experiences, our feelings, and impressions from various times of our lives.

After the fifteen minutes were up, we would each read aloud what we had written. More than once, I was moved to tears by the stories they shared. There were stories of childhood joys and traumas, war experiences, kindnesses never forgotten, unrequited love, and one man's dream of becoming a clown. I was deeply impressed with the beauty of the imagery they conjured with their words and the variety of experiences we collectively had. None of us were professional writers, yet the soulful, funny, and lyrical words spilled out from our handwritten pages like a swollen river overflowing its banks. We all had important, beautiful stories to tell.

As you write your legacy letter, let your stories spill over and fall upon the paper. Your words, your voice, your handwriting will all be important mementos of your life. Author Ray Bradbury reminds us that we should all leave something of ourselves behind for the people we know. In his famous book *Fahrenheit 451*, the character Granger tells Montag:

"Everyone must leave something behind when he dies, my grandfather said. A child or a book or a painting or a house or a wall built, or a pair of shoes made. Or a garden planted. Something your hand touched someway so your soul has somewhere to go when you die, and when people look at that tree or that flower you planted, you're there."[70]

In 2019, award-winning author Tim O'Brien wrote a book for his sons called *Dad's Maybe Book*. O'Brien had become a father in his mid- and late fifties and became concerned that he would not live long enough for his two sons to know who he was and what he believed in. He wrote: "I've always wished my dad had left for me what I am trying to leave for my kids in this book, just to say, 'I love you,' 'I'm proud of you.'" O'Brien's book is essentially a long legacy letter, sharing his experiences, advice, and thoughts about life and death.[71] What an incredible gift he gave to his sons and to the rest of us.

Please wait no longer. Take out that piece of paper, set the clock, and get writing. You have a chance to leave something of yourself behind. While each life is sadly finite, legacy letters are one small artifact of our lives that can endure for generations to come.

A Letter to the Future: The Time Capsule Letter

Imagine that one hundred years from now, the neighborhood you live in is undergoing a revitalization project. Old houses are being remodeled and made new for young families. Your old house is one of the first to get a facelift. The backhoe arrives and begins to tear down a wall of the house.

In the process of digging and clearing, a construction worker notices something shiny half-buried in the pile of rubbish by the old driveway. She walks over, wondering if it is just her imagination. But no, there is something long and metallic there. Upon further investigation, she finds a foot-long metal cylinder, pitted with rust and half-coated with dirt. It looks quite old and piques her curiosity immediately. With the help of a colleague, she carefully opens the old metal cylinder to reveal what is inside.

The cylinder holds several items, including a letter you wrote this year, some stamps, an assortment of coins, a small toy, a photograph of your family, a map of the city, your favorite poem, and a magazine from the same year. All of it is in remarkable condition, except for a few water stains on the letter's envelope. No one has touched these contents in more than a century. Her heart pounds faster. She thinks about how much the world has changed in that time. *Who,* she wonders, *put this time capsule together? Why did they create it and leave it in this way?* She looks quickly at the letter and capsule contents, puts the capsule aside for the moment, and returns to work.

Later, on her lunch hour, the construction worker returns to the time capsule to examine it more carefully. She sits back on the construction equipment with a sandwich in one hand and your letter in the other. She begins reading. She notices that the letter is quite detailed, including the following information:

1. The date you wrote the letter.
2. A friendly introduction saying who you are and why you decided to create this time capsule for a stranger.
3. The names of your family and their occupations.
4. The year in which the house was built, the names of any owners who had it before you, how long you owned it, and any changes you made to the house.
5. You tell the finder a bit about the biggest news of the day. Perhaps you even include a copy of the front page of the newspaper. Your letter might also discuss the things that are trending across the country at that moment, the names of the world leaders, the name of your city's mayor, the population of your city or town, and so on.
6. You describe your happiest memories of being in your home.
7. You write a few paragraphs about your current hopes and dreams for the future for you, your community, and the world.

8. You also include a description of what you think the world might be like in one hundred years.

9. You end by sending good wishes to the finder.

10. You bid them good-bye and good health.

Through your written words, you are now becoming acquainted. She is thrilled to have this memento of your family in the palm of her hand, delighting in the small gifts you sent into the future. She smiles at the playful nature of your offering. And there, across the decades of human history, you are now connected, just for a moment in time, heart to heart and soul to soul. Time momentarily stands still.

A Real Y2K Time Capsule Awaits Discovery

Many of us can remember the exciting days that led up to the new millennium in 2000. People around the world held exuberant celebrations to mark this auspicious event. My sister, a professional artist and art teacher, was also intrigued with the idea of marking the new millennium with a ritual of some kind. She settled on creating a Y2K time capsule and a late-night celebration on December 31, 1999, in her backyard to ceremoniously bury the filled capsule. "I wanted to put our family of four, our brother, and his son into the future somehow," she says. "It was for the same reason I create art, I suppose. You hope there will be something of you left behind for posterity—it's the kind of forward-thinking, legacy-building activity that I love."

Inside this time capsule, she placed several vials of local plant seeds, a sample of their city water, coins, a piece of her handmade jewelry, a photo of everyone at her backyard Y2K celebration, and a letter to the future. At precisely midnight of January 1, 2000, they dropped the sealed capsule into the hole they had dug in the yard, covered it with soil, and toasted the new millennium.

When my sister and her husband sold that home several years later, she created a map showing the time capsule's location and included it in a home journal she left for the next owners. She's hoping that this home journal will be passed along to subsequent owners and that in one hundred years or before, someone will try to locate and unearth the time capsule. As they open the small, stainless-steel container, they will meet her family for the first time, read their letter of introduction, and enjoy the trinkets and mementos inside.

Using her efforts as inspiration, I recently created my own time capsule when we remodeled our basement rec room. After a great deal of thought, we decided to seal and then cover over a quirky fireplace with drywall, but not before I put a cedar box filled with mementos and a letter in the firebox for someone to find someday. What fun it was deciding what to include in the box. It gave me a kick thinking about who might find that box years into the future. Will it be ten, fifty, one hundred years from now? If the box is discovered one day, we will all be there, represented by our pictures and our writing, ready to greet them.

A time capsule and letter are the vehicles for time travel. Your words on paper are the handshake through space and time. Please consider creating your own time capsule. Find an appropriate place to bury or leave it. Then imagine how it will feel when someone receives your gift far into the future. And you can imagine the smiles and delight right here, right now.

Letters Inspire Art

Artful Flourishes We Don't Forget

For thousands of years, human beings have found great joy in both giving and receiving gifts. Gift-giving can have many purposes: to honor someone at an important time or event, to show caring, to acknowledge the important role someone plays in your life, to curry favors, to express our deepest feelings for another, and more.

While each culture has its own traditions and expectations around gift-giving, the art of giving gifts is an important part of strengthening and reinforcing the social connections that bind us.

In the United States, where I live, people are expected to follow a few common conventions, such as wrapping the gift prior to presenting it to someone. This involves procuring the right wrapping paper or gift bag and carefully adorning the wrapped package with ribbons, bows, and other embellishments, then including a gift note or card. We know from research that gift recipients in our country are happier with gifts wrapped in attractive paper than one given in a brown paper bag, for example.[72] The goal is to conceal your gift in a package that will please the eye, show that you care, and create a bit of suspense and anticipation before it is opened. It is the small stuff, like taking the time to wrap a beautiful package, that makes life artful, more joyful, and satisfying.

I will always remember the exacting way my mother wrapped presents. First, she chose the wrapping paper carefully, with the recipient in mind. Once home, she cut, creased, and wrapped the paper around the gift box with quiet precision. Next, she lovingly crafted a bow from loose ribbon and attached it to the box with great care. All this effort was simply an extension of the love she showed us in many other ways.

Write a Letter, Give a Gift

When we write a letter, we are giving a gift of significant value: a one-of-a-kind, highly personalized present that no one else can duplicate or buy at a shopping mall. Because it is such a unique offering, handwritten letters deserve the same special treatment as any other gift. If we have the time and use our creativity, we can make our letters as enticing and appealing as a bejeweled gift box. We can do simple things to make them more fun or make them into a museum-worthy work of art. A lot will depend on your mood, time constraints, budget, and so on.

If I don't have much time, I still try to make my letters more fun by enclosing them in an attractive greeting card, adding colorful stickers, or affixing inexpensive vintage stamps to the envelope. Or explore these other ways to make a letter a feast for the eyes:

Practice Your Calligraphy (However Badly)

The art of calligraphy can take your letter writing to the next level. Calligraphy, which means "beautiful writing," can add drama and splendor to any letter. There are tens of thousands of fonts in the world, and many are so lovely they will stop you in your tracks. Calligraphy is a magnificent art form few people truly master. It takes concentration and persistence to form the curving letters and

inky flourishes smoothly and effortlessly. Even so, there is room for amateurs like you and me to play around with ink and paper, just for the fun of it.

The art of calligraphy humbles me. As a beginner learning this new skill, I could not help but have a deep respect for the earliest scribes, who had only crude vellum and basic writing tools to work with yet managed to create stunning illuminated texts and religious documents we still marvel at today. Ink smudges and lettering mistakes must have felt like a disaster; the calligrapher might have had to begin all over again, or at the very least, cleverly disguise their errors.

I acquired a deep appreciation for this art form when I took a beginner's calligraphy class. One week, the teacher told us to write out a four-line poem of our choosing, using the famous italic font. Four lines of a poem—simple, right? Wrong! I cannot tell you how many times I allowed my mind to wander for a split second, causing tiny errors over and over. Flawlessly copying text takes the same steely determination and focus that a painter or sculptor must apply to their artistic works. It is not easy; however, the outcome can be worth the struggle.

Imagine yourself going to the mailbox, where you find a letter addressed to you in ink, using the loveliest and most elegant font. The letters flow across the paper in a formal, majestic manner. Right then and there, time stops. Your chin drops, knees buckle, and a smile erupts on your face. You stand captivated by the artistry and the elegance of the script. There, in your hand, is a one-of-a-kind creation—a piece of art you won't be tossing into the wastebasket any time soon. In fact, you will be showing it to everyone you know and finding just the right place to showcase this artwork in your home. Perhaps it should be displayed next to the sepia-colored photographs of your great-aunt Margaret.

This lovely gift and your great-aunt Margaret's photograph show us that one-of-a-kind things are the most special gifts of all.

Postage Stamps

A book of many volumes would be necessary to do justice to the postage stamp. These marvelous little creations have delighted, fascinated, and brought joy to millions of people for more than 170 years. While stamps help us fulfill the mundane task of moving a letter from point A to point B, they add great visual interest to an otherwise dull, ho-hum piece of correspondence.

Countries take great pains to design stamps that bring attention to things of national significance, including native species, history, pop culture, holidays, famous or iconic figures, national parks, historic events, and even charitable causes. The variety of people and subjects they depict ensures that people of all ages around the world continue to find something that interests them. I often affix old, uncanceled stamps on my letters (available online) just for fun and because they are historically and graphically so interesting to look at.

Our national love affair with stamps inspired NASA to place one inside the New Horizons spacecraft when it made a flyby of Pluto in July 2015. According to Guinness World Records, no other postage stamp has ever traveled farther, more than three billion miles.[73]

Sealing Wax and Seals

Pirates used it, kings and queens used it, and of course, the aristocracy used it, too. In fact, for hundreds of years, anyone who wrote a letter depended on it not only to securely seal a letter or an envelope to prevent tampering but also to identify its authentic author. I am speaking, of course, about the wax seals that adorned important letters of times past.

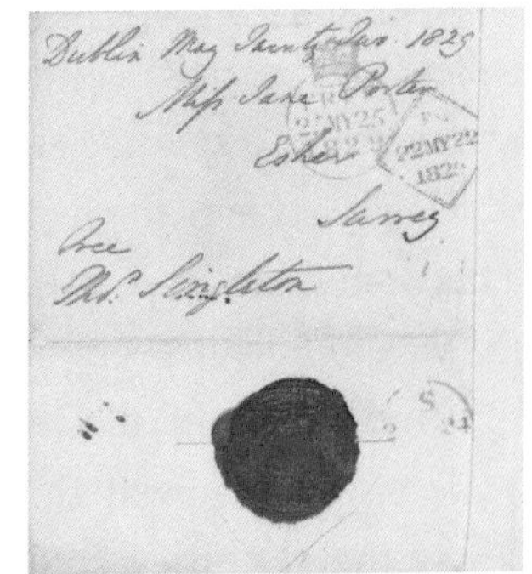

Sealing wax is a material that dries hard, forming a bond between wax and paper that is quite difficult to tamper with. For hundreds of years, a letter or envelope sealed with wax ensured that prying eyes could not determine the contents inside. This imperfect, irregular, yet elegant blob of wax over the back of an envelope or folded document was carefully affixed, impressed with an official seal or signet ring, and handed off to a courier for delivery. The signet ring's impression in wax became an essential method for proving who wrote an important letter or document.[74]

The wax seal gives the letter gravitas—a sense that something of great importance is in one's hand. Today, we have pre-glued envelopes to seal our letters in. Wax seals are no longer a necessity, to be sure. Yet when a letter arrives in our mailboxes today with a lovely wax seal affixed to it, we instantly appreciate the beauty of this time-honored practice. The romantics among us understand that while the wax is unnecessary today, it still has a sensory value—a beauty and feel worthy of our efforts even now.

The history of sealing wax is quite fascinating. The earliest examples of seals were in use in the Indus Valley and Mesopotamian civilizations from 3300 BCE to 150 BCE. The first seals were made of clay and stamped with rings or cylinders.[75] Later, Romans created their seals using bitumen.

In the Middle Ages, sealing wax was made of a mix of beeswax and Venice turpentine, a resinous extract of the European larch tree. At first, sealing wax was uncolored. Later, the wax got its characteristic deep red hue from vermilion, a dense red pigment made by grinding a powder of cinnabar (mercury sulfide).[76]

Wax formulas changed during the sixteenth century, each including various amounts of shellacs, resins, turpentine, chalk or plaster, and colorant. Today, most sealing wax comes in sticks or pellets and is available in a rainbow of colors. The stick or pellets are melted in a spoon or from a wax stick using a flame. The melted wax is placed over the flap of an envelope. While the wax is still soft, a decorative seal is pressed into the wax and then released, allowing the wax to fully harden.

In days of old, mail was hand-canceled and -carried, so wax seals easily survived the delivery process. When the recipient broke the seal, they could be confident that their letter had not been viewed by anyone else.[77] While most of us do not need wax to seal our envelopes, we may still want to embellish our letters with this extra flourish, just for the fun of it. Fortunately, new formulations of sealing wax allow us to easily indulge in this lovely, decorative art form.

Before mailing your letter, make certain to protect the seal from postal sorting machines by enclosing the letter inside another envelope. Be sure to account for the added weight of the wax or seal and the additional envelope when you affix postage. Or simply have the postal worker hand-cancel your special envelope and send your beautifully adorned letter on its way.

Embossed Seals

Paper embossing is another unique seal that can adorn a letter, card, or invitation. Embossing creates a raised impression on paper by placing a decorative die in contact with paper stock and then applying pressure.[78] Embossing leaves a design, pattern, or monogram slightly

raised above the surface of the paper. When you run your fingers over the embossed area, you can feel the design with your fingertips while also seeing it with the naked eye. Embossing literally adds another new dimension of elegance and sensuality to your correspondence.

Any or all of these small embellishments increase our sense of anticipation, take the art of letter writing to a whole new level of beauty, are guaranteed to please any recipient, and are sure to be remembered for a long time to come.

Doodles, Drawings, and Other Delights

Letters are sometimes known for having cheeky or sophisticated "traveling companions." Letter writers send these "companions" along with the letter as a special surprise, things like cartoons, bookmarks, drawings, tiny gifts and curiosities, photographs, items from nature, and other assorted oddities. The letter writer must be a bit creative when deciding what to include while also ensuring that it will survive the pitiless stamp-canceling process as it travels to its intended recipient.

The decision to insert surprise gifts inside a letter envelope comes with the desire to make the letter more fun, whimsical, and delightful. Who among us does not love a surprise, no matter how small? The best things, after all, often come in small packages.

What special gift, bit of humor, or touch of whimsy can you enclose in your next letter? Imagine the possibilities.

Doodles Always Delight

"Put down that pencil." "Stop drawing!" "Listen up and pay attention!" Most of us have undoubtedly heard these commands at some point during our school years or even in the workplace. Doodling has long been frowned upon. Teachers and bosses consider it the activity of slouches and slackers. And what a shame that is because we now know that it is often a precursor to the creation of polished, artistic, and highly original ideas.

Doodles are an unfiltered, authentic expression of someone's creativity. Research has shown that doodling is positively associated with better concentration, learning, creativity, and performance. It helps people to plan, multitask, and open new avenues of thinking.[79] So why, then, do we downplay its value and importance? If we can't doodle in schools and workplaces, what better place to have a go at it than in the privacy of our own homes when writing letters?

Bringing the doodling mindset to letter writing is a great gift to the letter's recipient. It adds a significant degree of whimsy and originality to the practice. A piece of stationery is a blank canvas that doodlers may find hard to resist. Your doodling capabilities can show an unknown side of you. In between the lines—and in the margins, perhaps—an entirely different portrait of you might emerge, bringing new dimension and complexity to others' understanding of who you are. How lovely is that?

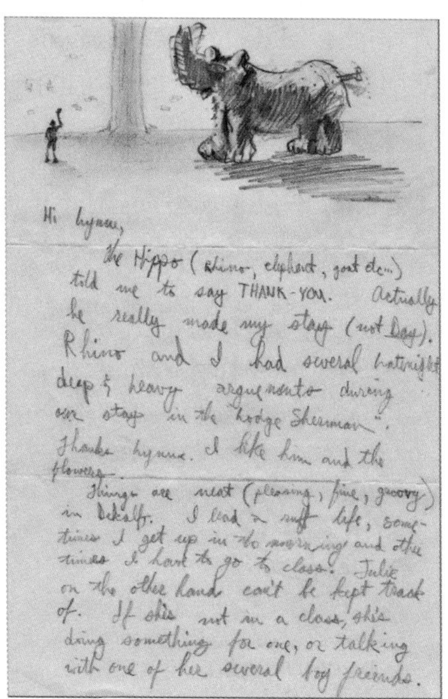

Hi Lynne,

The Hippo (rhino, elephant, goat etc...) told me to say THANK-YOU. Actually he really made my stay (not Day). Rhino and I had several late-night deep & heavy arguments during our stay in the "Lodge Sherman". Thanks Lynne. I like him and the flowers.

Things are neat (pleasing, fine, groovy) in Dekalb. I lead a soft life, sometimes I get up in the morning and other times I have to go to class! Julie on the other hand can't be kept track of. If she's not in a class, she's doing something for one, or talking with one of her several boy friends.

Original Art Tucked Inside

Imagine that one day you open a letter from someone you hold dear and tucked inside the envelope you find a special surprise: a tiny watercolor painting along with their letter. The painting is a quickly rendered self-portrait the artist hopes you will keep and remember them by. You feel deeply touched and honored by their gift, immediately pinning the portrait to the corkboard by your desk.

If you are very lucky, letters will sometimes include unique artful creations like this. Creative works, like artwork, have great intrinsic value on their own, but they mean a great deal more to us when we know that they have been made for us alone. There is a deep understanding that art is tied to expression, emotion, and love. And for this reason, we find it hard to part with handmade art, whether it is a simple line drawing, an expressive letter, or both.

As I was helping my husband sort through some of his mother's belongings after she passed away, we found her carefully curated book of stamps from the 1930s and 1940s. On the inside back cover of the book, I found two old letters secured with yellowing strips of adhesive tape. My husband had never seen them before, so we decided to remove them to find out why they had been singled out for preservation. One letter was from a Scottish cousin serving in the Royal Air Force during World War II. The other, a letter from a dear brother, Don, serving in the US Coast Guard during the same war.

Opening Don's letter, we found a charming birthday poem he had written for his kid sister back home. Above the poem, he drew a pretty bouquet of flowers. His sweet poetry combined with his talent for art clearly made this letter something very special to my mother-in-law. So much so that she preserved it carefully in a safe place for seventy-five years. This gift cost Don nothing to give but clearly meant the world to his sister thousands of miles away. Because she could not part with it, we, the next generation and beyond, can appreciate it, too.

Artful Drawings Tucked Inside Letters Become Famous Children's Stories

Did you know that Beatrix Potter's famous book *The Tale of Peter Rabbit* had its beginnings in a series of letters sent to a young child?

While communicating with her childhood governess in the late 1800s, Beatrix decided to include some whimsical little stories and watercolor paintings for her governess to read to her small children. Not surprisingly, the children fell in love with the stories and wanted to read them again and again. At the urging of her former governess, Beatrix formed the stories into a series of books for young children. *The Tale of Peter Rabbit* debuted to great acclaim in 1901, and the rest is history.[80] More than one hundred years later, her books are still highly popular in the world of children's literature.

Imagine if Beatrix had never tucked these treasured stories inside her letters. It seems likely that we would have never had these charming stories to read to our young ones at bedtime. What a tragic loss it would have been for the generations of children to come!

Photographs

When I open letters, I am usually expecting only to see words on paper, which themselves are a delight. However, it is always a bonus to find a photo or two tucked inside the letter. While letters provide a sensory experience of their own, photographs offer another way to delight our senses. Even in the days of real-time, instant communication, a physical photograph is a timeless gift. No need to first run to our printers to make the print. Instead, we can immediately frame or pin it on the wall or include it in an album or journal. It also helps that someone else has selected and reproduced it for us, leaving us to simply enjoy it.

Doodads

Once, when I was going through a trying medical situation, a kind friend, Beth, sent me a get-well card. When I opened the card, a spring-wound paper butterfly flew from my hand and danced around the room for a few seconds before dropping to the floor. This tiny butterfly gave me quite a surprise, which brought a smile to my face during a difficult experience. I adore letters and cards for this reason. We are never too old for these thoughtful surprises.

You can be creative with the things you tuck inside your letters.

Every now and then, a letter will arrive in your mailbox that has some unusual heft or thickness to it. Right away, the anticipation builds as soon as you notice it among the bills and junk mail. You wonder what in the world could be inside the envelope. Sometimes, the envelope simply includes a long letter requiring many sheets of stationery. But other times, an unusually thick letter means that hidden treasure is included inside. There might be something unexpected like:

- newspaper clippings
- postcards
- recipes
- mementos

- bookmarks
- inspirational quotes
- origami cranes or other paper ephemera
- stamps, buttons, or pins
- bits of nature (seeds, dried flowers, leaves)
- a special coin
- puzzles, jokes

The sender knows that it is all about creating a sense of anticipation and surprise as you tear open the envelope. Sometimes, the smallest and least expensive gifts are the most special. Letters that include a few doodads are sure to lift the spirits of those you love, and these simple gestures will be remembered in their hearts for years to come.

Poetry

I have always admired the poets among us. I have never had the knack for expressing myself in this way, but I deeply appreciate those who take the time to develop a meaningful idea, impression, or message in a few words. Poets by nature are some of the most keenly observant and sensitive people around. If you have this knack for saying a great deal while using words sparingly, then, by all means, treat someone to your craft, whether it is a racy limerick, multi-stanza epic poem, a "roses are red" poem, or haiku.

On occasion, I have received poems carefully typed, using a pretty font, or handwritten on a separate piece of paper and tucked into the envelope accompanying a letter. I usually sit down and read the poem slowly so that I can savor the use of language and fully process the meaning of the words.

If your pen pal is a poet, you may be able to see another facet of their personality that may not be apparent from your normal casual conversations. Poetry gives us a special lens through which we can see their souls. There is no better gift than that. If you or your letter writing companion are not born poets, you can still share poetry by authors you admire. Sometimes, these inserts can arrive at just the right moment.

Some years ago, when my brother died, I was in shock and completely bereft. After his memorial service was over, my family decided to hold a small, private memorial for ourselves on my parents' farm when we could fulfill his last wish to have his ashes scattered there. I wanted to find something short to read that would honor my brother and bring some peace to the family. But what might that be? I couldn't think of anything appropriate. I felt completely inept.

A few days later, waiting for me in my mailbox was the solution to my problem. A close friend had tucked a poem she loved inside her sympathy card. I sat down and read the poem with a grateful heart and deep appreciation for her thoughtfulness.

Native American Poem, by Anonymous

I give you this one thought to keep—
I am with you still. I do not sleep.

I am a thousand winds that blow.
I am the diamond glints on snow.
I am the sunlight on ripened grain.
I am the gentle autumn rain.

When you awaken in the morning's hush,
I am the swift, uplifting rush
of quiet birds in circled flight.
I am the soft stars that shine at night.
Do not think of me as gone—
I am with you still in each new dawn.

Given my brother's and my family's love of nature, this was exactly the poem I needed for our private ceremony. Reading it aloud added meaning to a heartbreaking event. It is never easy to find the right words in the middle of tragedy or loss. However, poems can often convey the sentiments we cannot. What a gift to find this fitting tribute to my brother included inside her special card.

A Bit of Nature Tucked Inside

Letters offer a fun way to send someone a souvenir from the far-off places you have visited. Interesting mementos can be tucked inside an envelope. Perhaps it is a paper menu from a favorite restaurant, a cocktail umbrella from your dinner cruise, a ticket stub from the Eiffel Tower. You can get creative and give your friends and family members a unique surprise.

While visiting Sanibel Island in Florida, I decided that it would be fun to send a bit of the beach to my father and sister, both still stuck in the Midwest's wintry weather. I bought two cards, both with illustrations of the shells of Sanibel. Inside the envelope, I included some very tiny, empty shells and a bit of sand collected on the beach. It's true that some of the shells did not survive the trip through the postal sorters, but some did. (Do be aware of additional postage required for extra weight and write *Please Hand-Cancel* on your envelope.) Nonetheless, it was a fun way to bring a bit of the ocean to their cold and snowy homes.

When my mother, my sister, and I visited my grandmother's birthplace in Scotland, my mother carefully picked a few sprigs of heather she found near her mother's ancestral home and pressed them in a travel guide to protect them until she returned home. Once properly dried, she inserted these heather sprigs inside the letters she sent to my two sisters who were unable to join us on the trip. One sister laminated that sprig of heather and hung it on her office wall, where it still is today.

Visiting New Hampshire one fall, I was inspired to collect and press the vibrantly colored leaves I found everywhere, as well as small bits of fallen birch bark, to save for a future card or letter. The items you select can be natural and organic—something precious to us, ubiquitous or ephemeral. They are hints of the beauty we are experiencing and want to share with those unable to see it for themselves.

Receiving these modest offerings inside a letter can be especially meaningful to those who must live inside a good deal of the time. Just be certain that what you collect and send is not from a state or national park or is not an invasive, rare, threatened, or endangered species. Also, be mindful of sending seeds and plants across state and international borders; check with the US Department of Agriculture to determine current regulations.

Cartoons

Many of us know a perennial cynic, political junkie, humorist, or social commentator. Some of them have a knack for writing political satire. Others may have the rare ability to share their offbeat, amusing perspectives in the form of a cartoon. Admittedly, these folks are rare, but I have known people capable of making serious things very humorous. They make me laugh out loud—even when I want to despair. Perhaps you are one of the fortunate souls who've received handmade cartoons or other humorous writings from one of these rare individuals. Lucky you! While I am not known for my great wit, I certainly treasure the people in my life who are known for theirs.

If you wish you had the talent of cartoonists but don't, clip some cartoons you especially like and tuck them into the envelope along with your letter. Everyone appreciates a good laugh, and you will be doing your part to lift someone's spirits.

Inspirational Quotes

Fortunately, there is no shortage of brilliant, thoughtful philosophers, religious leaders, writers, politicians, and average anonymous folks who speak or write eloquently, generating quotable quotes for the rest of us to enjoy. I must confess, I have always enjoyed pithy, meaningful quotes. They have brought me great solace and inspiration during difficult, gut-wrenching situations and confusing times in my life.

If you are good at identifying inspiring quotes that can touch a heart or provide the wisdom someone might need, do include one in your next letter. That same friend might one day decide to rewrite that quote in beautiful calligraphy and send it to another of their good friends "just because." Sometimes, things show up for us at precisely the right time and with a mysterious synchronicity that astonishes us.

Letters That Think Outside the Envelope

Of all the things people might call me, *avant-garde* would *not* be one of them. I have always been rather conservative in the way I dress and decorate my home. I have not been known for doing wild and crazy things in my life. However, as safe and predictable as I may be in certain areas of my life, I have always been interested in looking beyond the status quo, trying new ideas, and getting creative when it seems like the more expedient, joyful, or rewarding thing to do.

Because I am more of an observer than an artist, I must sometimes live vicariously through the lives of the more daring and edgy souls around me. Creativity is truly a remarkable thing, and I never cease to be amazed by those who see only new possibilities when they look around. So when I discovered that there are artists who have reimagined the letter in new, outstandingly creative ways, I had to dig deeper.

If I say the word *letter*, most people automatically imagine a traditional rectangular white envelope, affixed with one stamp in the upper-right corner and neatly addressed on the center or lower-right portion of the envelope. But why not think outside the envelope? We do not need to settle for the bland and predictable all the time. Some people have pushed the edge of the envelope with these innovative and interesting alternatives.

(Note: If you wish to try some or all of these ideas, please have the post office weigh your letter before affixing postage, as all these options will probably cost you more to send than a standard letter).

1. **Nature Mail.** Write a letter using natural materials for paper—a piece of birch bark, for example, where you can write a short letter, roll it up, and secure it with twine before posting. Be thoughtful about where you procure your birch bark. No peeling off tree bark in local, state, or national parks, or trespassing, please!

2. **Fly Me to the Moon.** Affix your letter to a small, beautiful kite.

3. **Go Nuts!** On your next vacation to the Caribbean, send your true love a hulled coconut. Write your short "letter" on the shell.

4. **Send a Very Tiny Letter.** For a small charge, an online mail service will send a very tiny letter, along with a very tiny magnifying glass, through the mail to your recipient.[81]

5. **Create a Folded Paper Surprise.** Write your letter on an origami paper animal and give your loved one a special surprise.

6. **Send a Letter in a Bottle.** Sending a clear plastic bottle with a beautifully addressed letter and other surprises inside would surely bring smiles.

7. **Post an "Eggceptional" Letter.** Fit a tiny letter inside a plastic or papier-mâché Easter egg and seal with clear

tape. Your loved ones will be egg-static when it arrives in their mailbox.

8. **Knots About You.** Cut a piece of wood veneer or scrap of lumber into a shape—your choice!—and write a message on one side and the address for the recipient on the other. Create a wood-burned scene on the wood if you are feeling especially creative.

9. **Tintype Letters.** Find an antique or decorative food tin and insert your letter inside. Seal the opening with clear packing tape.

10. **Drinks Are on Me!** Use a bar coaster as a postcard.

These are but a few ideas to encourage you to think outside the envelope and provide a bit of delight for someone in your life.

Mail Art

It's a marvelous art form, the letter—full of wonder and surprise.[82]

—*Ray Johnson*

Happily, many artists today are taking letters and postcards to new heights. Envelopes and postcards are the canvas. Artists make these canvases come alive.

Mail art—also known as *postal art* and *correspondence art*—is a populist artistic genre that focuses on sending small-scale art through the postal service. The genre was created in the 1950s by Ray Johnson's New York Correspondence School and by the Fluxus movement, which still exists today.[83]

In contemporary times, mail artists create a variety of forms, including decorated letters and postcards, paper, collages, recycled materials, images, and stamps, but they can also incorporate music, sound art, poetry, or anything else that the artist wants to include. Once officially mailed, the creations become mail art. Enthusiasts tout the importance of mail art because it provides a more even

The possibilities for creating beauty on the face of an envelope are endless.

playing field for artists, given that no jury's approval is required to get a piece into an exhibition. Thus, artists can circumvent the less formal art market, distribution, and exhibition channels. Mail artists are now relying more on websites, social media, and blog posts to share their works with the wider world, with numerous websites devoted to this unique art form.

Mail art is created by anyone for anyone, no art credentials required. Envelopes become public expressions of creativity, seen and appreciated in a somewhat random, unplanned way, although you can also view them in museums and galleries around the world.

In truth, mail art has probably been going on for a very long time in a more informal and largely unorganized manner. If you go back through old letters, you can find amateur artists that included fun or beautiful art on the outside of envelopes or inside on the stationery.

Thinking Outside the Envelope

If we adjust our paradigms a bit, the envelope can be more than a dull, hardworking shroud of paper that surrounds correspondence. Rather, it has great potential to be a playful space where colorful drawings, paintings, and calligraphy blend in dramatic style, where playful sketches or random images can dance unfettered across an envelope's front or back, or where original stamp creations can take center stage in a visually interesting way.

Envelopes become a place to create an unusual focal point for spirited creations if we choose to take advantage of the opportunity. Let's challenge ourselves to have more fun and think outside the envelope!

Epistolary Art

In addition to letters being art forms, they can spark other art forms, too. Take, for example, the epistolary genre of writing.

The word *epistolary* is derived from the Greek word *epistole*, which means *letter*. Epistolary is a genre of writing where the author uses letters, journals, newspaper clippings, emails, diary entries, and so on as the means to tell or embellish a story.[84]

This unusual literary tool allows a book's characters to express their own feelings and relay their own stories through the letters they write to other characters in a story. The author does not tell us directly what they want us to know about a character. Instead, we are allowed to explore this for ourselves through the characters' own words. Letters let us see inside the characters' minds to a greater degree.

For hundreds of years (since the 1600s, in fact), dozens of novels and plays have been written using the epistolary style. Some famous examples include:[85]

- *The Color Purple* by Alice Walker
- *Frankenstein* by Mary Shelley
- *Dracula* by Bram Stoker

- *Pamela* by Samuel Richardson
- *Persuasion* and *Pride and Prejudice* by Jane Austen
- *84 Charing Cross Road* by Helene Hanff
- *Griffin and Sabine: An Extraordinary Correspondence* by Nick Bantock
- *Dear Committee Members* by Julie Schumacher
- *The Guernsey Literary and Potato Peel Pie Society* by Mary Ann Shaffer and Annie Barrows
- *The White Tiger* by Aravind Adiga

Epistolary Plays

Letters can also be the springboard or foundation for telling a story onstage. For example, in 2020, the community in Hopkins, Minnesota, produced an original musical play with peace as its theme. Entitled *Peace 4 the Ages*, the cast consisted of twenty-eight people ranging in age from eleven to eighty-seven.

To create the musical, the play's producers paired elderly cast members with youthful counterparts and asked them to begin a pen pal correspondence. Each participant had to exchange three letters with their partner. After the exchange of letters, the pen pals met in person. The process was a meaningful way for the pairs to get to know one another and to allow each other to explore what the word *peace* meant to them.

"The farther with the letters we got, the more articulate we got and the more truthful he got," a seventy-five-year-old participant says of her fifteen-year-old pen pal.[86] At the end of the letter-writing process, the letters became very personal and intimate.[87] It is noteworthy that some of the participants had never handwritten a letter before this experience.

The musical play was created based on its cast's letters and the interactions. Letters created the platform for the generation of ideas as well as the trust in one another's ability to cocreate a powerful play intended to provoke thinking about peace, age, and having a voice.[88]

Other famous plays have used letters as the backdrop for their plots, including *Love Letters* by A. R. Gurney. Letters are excellent as inspiration for a unique form of storytelling. They provide the means for creating memorable characters, building intriguing plotlines, and telling a story from a unique perspective.

Letters Center Stage

In recent years, letters (unaltered, unvarnished) have become the focus of another kind of theatrical art. A unique form of entertainment called Letters Live was first produced in England, then later moved across the Atlantic to sell-out crowds. The goal of the show's producers was to increase literacy. The performers for Letters Live read aloud letters of notable artists, musicians, actors, historical figures, and so on in front of a live audience. The kind of letters vary enormously, including those written by Gandhi, Elvis Presley, Sojourner Truth, David Bowie, Janis Joplin, Kurt Vonnegut, and Abraham Lincoln. The apparent popularity of these events shows the public's yearning to engage with authentic, humorous, and meaningful forms of expression. That is good news for the future of letters.

Letter Writing as the Subject for Fine Art

Let us not forget that many studio artists have included letter writing as the subject of their paintings or drawings. Artists interested in capturing the daily activities of everyday people find ample inspiration in capturing writing as a painting. Consider a few examples of famous mail-related paintings or drawings now seen in museums around the world:

- Gerard ter Borch, *Woman Writing a Letter*, 1655
- Johannes Vermeer, *A Lady Writing*, 1665
- Thomas Benjamin Kennington, *Reading the Letter*, 1885

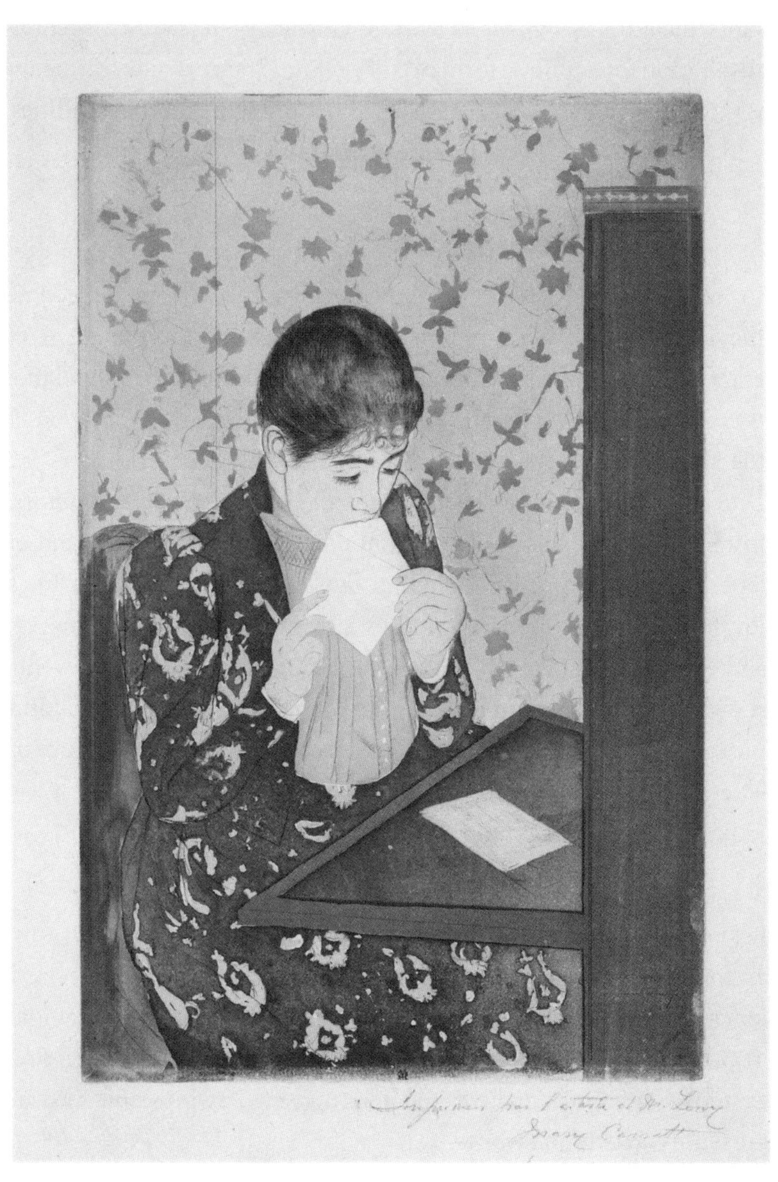

An example of an epistolary fine art painting by Mary Cassatt.

- Vincent van Gogh, *Portrait of the Postman Joseph Roulin*, 1888
- Mary Cassatt, *The Letter*, 1890-1891
- Edward Hopper, *New York Office*, 1962

This is but a small example of the artists who found the act of letter writing inspiring, leaving us with a whole new set of artistic creations to color our days. Letters enable the expression of creativity in myriad forms, and we are all the richer for it.

The Curious, Quirky, and Fascinating World of Letter Writing

A Short History of the Letter

The history of human civilization—at least twenty-five hundred years of it—is closely linked to the history of the handwritten letter. It is impossible to calculate the impact that letters have had on expanding and advancing societies, including the development of written languages and the arts, supporting social movements, sharing scientific findings, enabling commerce, spreading religions, creating new philosophies, and connecting people in new and sophisticated ways.

Old letters are found in many places, including attics, libraries, museums, archives, bottles, strongboxes, sunken ships, time capsules, under the floorboards, and more. Their survival and preservation have allowed us to know a great deal more about ourselves and our societies—the good, the bad, and the ugly—than we ever could have without them. Their importance to historians and societies is utterly incalculable.

Interesting Historical Facts

Long before the English derived the word *letter*, humans had been busy creating the means and the tools necessary to send communications. Letter writing as we know it today required myriad inventions and revolutionary technologies across millennia. Each incremental improvement in these tools made it easier for civilizations to develop.

Imagine the frustration that must have existed for thousands of years when all humans had to work with were crude instruments like animal bones and heavy clay or stone tablets. What a revelation it must have been to use a lightweight reed pen and papyrus for the first time. Papyrus, invented in Egypt around 3,000 BCE, was a thick, relatively lightweight writing surface made by layering triangular-shaped wetland grass together, moistening them, and pressing them flat. Later, the reed pen was invented by sharpening hollow, relatively tough, tubular-shaped marsh grasses. Reed pens and papyrus revolutionized writing, moving, and storing human communications in significant ways.

It was not until the year 500 BCE that a woman named Queen Atossa of Persia wrote the first known handwritten letter.[89] She never imagined, I'm certain, that her letter would change human history.

The timeline that follows highlights some of the key innovations made over thousands of years that enabled the creation of handwritten letters as we now know them. I tip my hat to the many inventors who wanted to find easier and better ways to communicate and could not leave well enough alone.

Timeline of Key Innovations

Before Common Era (BCE)

- 3000 BCE—Egyptians master the art of making papyrus, the material used for writing hieroglyphics and pictograms. This material would remain in use for longer than any other material in the history of written documents.[90]

- 3000 BCE—Ink, made from carbon black, water, and animal glue, is invented in China.[91]
- 2450 BCE—Animal skins are used to make parchment/vellum paper.[92]
- 2000 BCE—Egyptians invent the reed pen. These early pens are made from the hollow, tubular stems of marsh grasses.[93]
- 590 BCE—Wood, metal, or bone pens are created. Papyrus is still the paper of choice for writing.[94]
- 575 BCE—The Roman emperor Claudius makes a new type of cross-layered papyrus, which is not as easily damaged by writing instruments.[95]
- 500 BCE—According to the ancient historian Hellanicus, Persian queen Atossa writes the first known letter.[96]

Common Era (CE)

- 105—Ts'ai Lun invents paper in China.[97]
- Later 100s—Inventor Cai Lin refines paper production by making paper from heated wood chips, rags, cotton, and old fishnets.[98]
- 500—Bird feathers replace reed pens.[99]
- 600s—The quill pen is now in use and will continue to be used for the longest period in history (from the 600s to the 1800s). Europeans determine that the feathers from living swans, turkeys, and geese make the best pens.[100]
- 700s—Hindu-Malayan empires write legal documents on copper plates or scrolls and write other less important documents on more perishable media.
- 751—Arabs begin producing paper after they learn its "recipe" from Chinese prisoners.[101]
- 1109—Earliest use of paper in Europe.[102]
- 1151—Paper manufacturing begins in Europe.[103]

- 1200s—A great advance in writing material comes in the thirteenth century with the invention of paper made with linen rags.[104]
- 1300s—Cursive and lowercase letters are derived from italic calligraphy during the Renaissance period. Italic is the writing method of choice among some Europeans and Americans from this time forward.[105]
- 1639—First notice of the creation of a postal service in colonial America. Prior to this, colonists depended on friends, indigenous peoples, and merchants to deliver letters and other messages between colonies.[106]
- 1662—Graphite pencils are first mass-produced in Nuremberg, Germany.[107]
- 1775—Members of the Second Continental Congress appoint a postmaster general for the United States. The decision signals the birth of the Post Office Department, the predecessor of the US Postal Service and the second-oldest government department of the present United States.[108]
- 1822—John Mitchell from Birmingham, England, begins development of a machine-made steel-point pen on a mass scale. These are ink pens, functioning in the same way as the quill but sturdier and much less expensive.[109]
- 1827—Romanian inventor Petrache Poenaru receives the first patent for the invention of a fountain pen. His design proves to be problematic, however, limiting its production.[110]
- Pre-1840—Letters are delivered by courier, coach, or a horseback rider. The person who receives the letter must pay for the letter. The cost depends upon the number of pages and how far it has traveled.[111]
- 1840—Great Britain introduces the first prepaid stamp nationwide postal delivery service, with the Penny Black stamp (portrait of the young Queen Victoria) for letters less than half

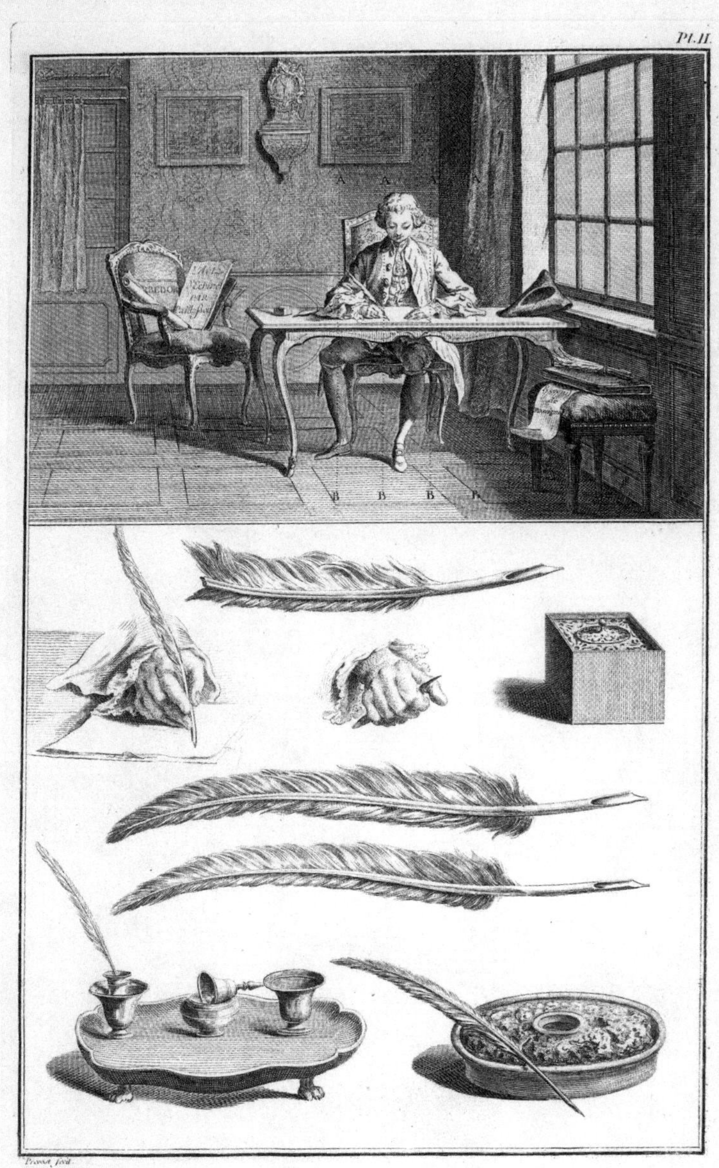
Pl.II.
Art d'Ecrire.

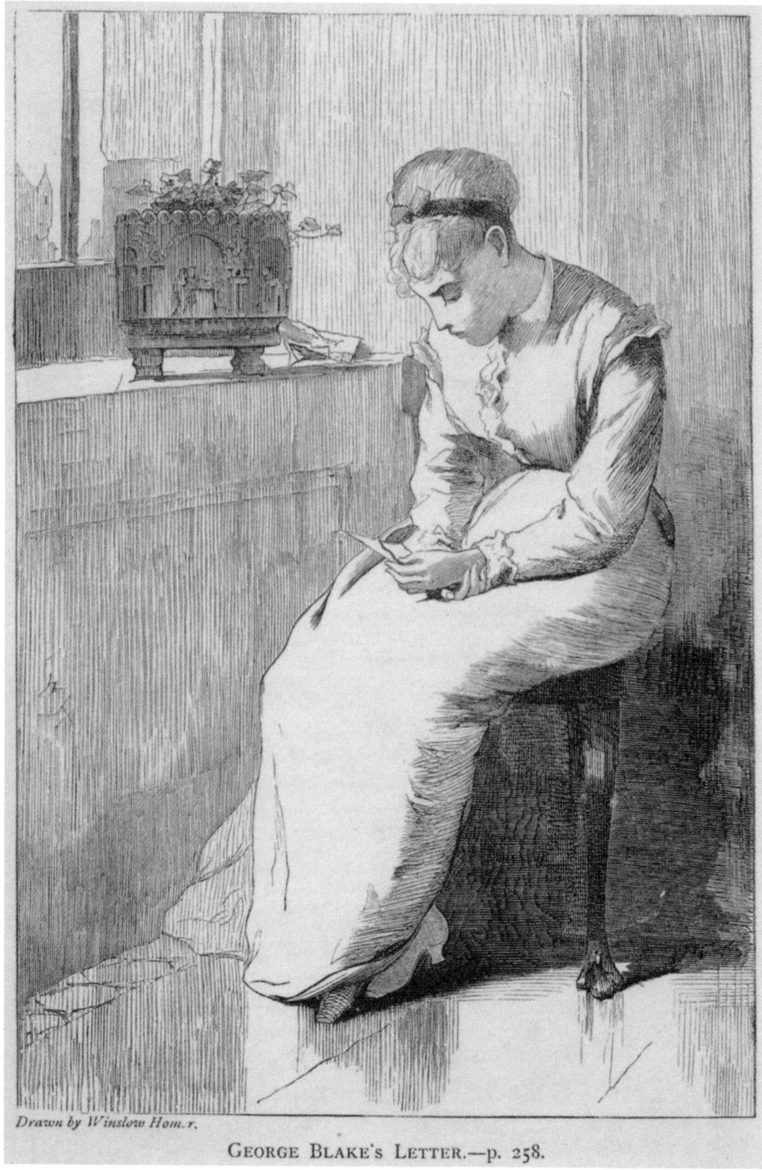

Drawn by Winslow Hom.r.

GEORGE BLAKE'S LETTER.—p. 258.

an ounce and the Two Penny Blue stamp for letters more than that weight. Other countries soon copy this idea.[112]

- 1842—The United States introduces a limited US Postal Service in August 1842.[113]

- 1844—Paper is manufactured on a large-scale basis, using ground wood as its main ingredient.[114]
- 1845—The United States creates a uniform five-cent postal charge for sending mail.[115]
- 1847—The United States creates its first standardized stamps for letters.[116]
- 1860–1861—In the United States, the Pony Express delivers letters, newspapers, and messages between Missouri and California using relays of horse-mounted riders. During its eighteen months of operation, it reduces the time it takes for messages to travel between the Atlantic and Pacific coasts to about ten days. The Pony Express is an important means of communication before construction of the transcontinental telegraph in 1861.[117]
- 1883—Lewis Edson Waterman develops and gains a patent for the three-channel ink feed fountain pen. This design ensures a smooth flow of ink to paper and soon revolutionizes writing.[118]
- 1888—American John J. Loud invents the first ballpoint pen. The ballpoint pen initiates a major turning point in the evolution of the pen.[119] Later, it is redesigned into a popular writing instrument.
- 1894—*The Palmer Guide to Business Writing* is published, providing lessons in practical penmanship.[120]
- 1918—US government begins first airmail deliveries between New York and Washington, DC. [121]
- 1933—László Bíró, a Hungarian journalist, patents a commercially successful ballpoint pen. His use of quick-drying ink and a small rotating metal ball keeps the pen from drying out and distributes the ink smoothly.[122]
- 1971—The first personal computer (KENBAK-1) is invented, setting the stage for a new way of communicating.[123]

- 1972—Steve Jobs, late founder of Apple Computers, audits a calligraphy class at Reed College. He becomes fascinated with typography and fonts. Ten years later, he develops the Macintosh computer and uses his keen interest in calligraphy to design attractive computer fonts. Personal computers begin replacing handwritten documents.[124]
- 1980s—The Rollerball pen, created by the Japanese company Ohto, hits the markets. This pen is followed by the felt-tipped pen developed by Yukio Hore.[125]

Paper for Posterity

In many parts of the world, paper is plentiful, affordable (at an environmental cost), and generally high quality. Paper can be both a simple necessity and a luxurious splurge. Regardless of which it is, we have become highly dependent on it—so much so that it remains a key to the success of commerce and the ease of our day-to-day lives. We still love paper, even though futurists of an earlier age predicted its demise long ago. The paperless office, touted as an inevitability with the invention of the computer, hasn't yet come to fruition in many places.

Hundreds of years of modifications and inventions have brought us to the sophistication of today's paper manufacturing and recycling processes. We can all rejoice in the abundant varieties of beautiful papers available today. For me, a trip to a stationery store is like a visit to the candy store. And I am equally weak in resisting temptation in both places. A letter on lovely paper is a sensory experience, but we should never forget what it takes to bring that gorgeous paper to our desks.

Each year, every person in the United States uses around 680 pounds of paper.[126] However, to provide that amount of paper to consumers, paper companies must cut down nearly two billion trees each year.[127] That is a staggering number that should give us all pause. We can reduce the number of trees cut down by using the many lovely, recycled stationeries and cards now available. This way, we not only leave an important written legacy but also a positive environmental legacy as well. Let's light the way when we can.

The Mighty Pen

Multiple inventors over time devoted themselves to perfecting the writing pen. In 1884, Lewis Waterman's version created an efficient ink feed system that allowed for the optimal exchange of ink and air as it delivered the ink to paper—and ushered in the modern-day fountain pen. Other American inventors include George S. Parker, of Parker Pen Company fame.

Interestingly, the humble fountain pen played a critical role in the escape of captured US troops in prisoner of war camps during World War II. Ingenious inventors found that fountain pens could be used to hold highly concentrated dyes instead of inks. These dyes allowed prisoners to create believable-looking civilian clothes or fake military uniforms from their prison uniforms. In fact, having discovered that the humble pen was such a useful escape aid, the military also magnetized them so that they could be used as compasses and created places for hiding tiny maps and medications for the prisoners lucky enough to escape.[128]

The pen has been a most impactful technology, despite its relative simplicity. It is easy to learn to love the ritual and the craft that a nice pen brings to creative work. When you use a pen, you automatically slow down, and your brain functions differently and more effectively compared to when you are typing on a computer. This is especially true in academic settings.[129]

People who enjoy writing with fountain pens often connect at a sensory level with the beautiful way the pen feels in the hand and moves smoothly across the stationery. Even today, some writers still exclusively use fountain pens and other quality pens in their day-to-day work, even if it means occasional ink-stained fingers or clothes.

Ink: Get It in Writing

Many ancient cultures independently created inks as a means of drawing and writing. The first use of inks was largely for artistic purposes, such as cave paintings. The first cave paintings were created in Spain and Indonesia around forty thousand years ago.[130] Later cave paintings, which include more sophisticated figurative imagery, were created around thirty-two thousand years ago, in the Chauvet Cave in France, using inks made with red, ochre, and black manganese dyes.[131]

The development of writing with ink began in Egypt as early as 2500 BCE using papyrus as the medium for sharing information. Inks were made of a type of carbon called *lamp black*, created by partially burning tar with a little vegetable oil.[132]

Chinese inks (India inks) were developed at approximately the same time but may go back as far as three or maybe four millennia to the late Chinese Neolithic period. India ink was made by combining carbon black, lamp black, and charred bones, combined with animal glue, which created a dried block that could be liquified by adding water.[133]

Because carbon-based inks were not ideal for every writing surface, an important innovation came to ink production in the eighth century. This new ink, called *iron gall ink*, required a chemical precipitation based on tannic acids and iron salts, bound by resin. This ink could be used with a quill pen on a greater variety of surfaces and was also more water resistant, making it the preferred ink from the twelfth century to the nineteenth century. Some artists still use iron gall inks today.[134]

Like the pen, ink is rarely given the respect it deserves. Inks allowed for the creation of art and literature, sharing revolutionary new ideas in the sciences, and perhaps most importantly, connecting human hearts separated by distance or circumstances. It is easy to forget just how long humans have used and relied upon ink to build civilizations and to transform and elevate our collective human experience.

Life in the Digital Age

I have read articles by people who adamantly declare that pen and paper are now "dead" as a means of communication—in other words, irrelevant in today's world. For computer and technology enthusiasts, the pen may be, in fact, irrelevant. But for those of us who have personal histories tied to the use of pen and paper or who want to keep the arts of cursive writing and handwritten letters alive, the pen still rules for special occasions or our most important personal correspondence.

It is true that the pen no longer serves the same role it once did. The printing press, typewriter, and then computers contributed to the pen's slow decline as the premiere tool for communication. Fortunately, however, despite the high-tech digital world of instant communication, the fountain pen continues to attract the attention of people from younger and older generations alike.

According to Troy Patterson, "The fountain pen *has not* gone the way of the horse and buggy. Rather, the correct analogy is with the horse itself: it would be peculiar to use one as your only mode of transportation, but it's a privilege to trot one out on special occasions."[135]

"The allure of handwriting is definitely creeping its way back into people's daily lives again," says Charles Huang, writer for *Tokyo Weekender*.[136] Apparently, this is no surprise for those in the pen manufacturing industry. Pen and other stationery products have seen a huge resurgence in sales and popularity in recent years. "People realized the value of analog after going all in on digital," according to Taizo Yamamoto, the CEO of an Osaka stationery brand, Yamamoto Papers.[137]

Kaoru Yamagishi, owner of Bungubox, a boutique fountain pen store in Omotesando, Japan, comments, "Humans are, by definition, analog. I think no matter how far digitalization advances, the human brain will still crave the analog . . . The human brain goes into full gear when we write with pen and paper."[138]

A carpenter purchases reliable, high-quality tools that will last. A musician seeks an instrument with which they can form a deep connection. The author grabs the pen that will make the writing experience a little more joyful, sensuous, and freeing. The tools we choose with which to engage in our creativity and artistry do matter. When we choose a writing implement, it is with the expectation of sharing something of our inner selves. With a wonderful pen in hand, this sharing can become more fluid and enjoyable.

If you want to invest in a quality pen, there are hundreds of choices in the marketplace. Will it be a vintage fountain pen? Solid gold? Bejeweled? An inexpensive but trusty disposable? You will find something to fit any budget. And it does not really matter which you select. What matters most is the enjoyment you get from combining your favorite pen, paper, and ink. The tools of expression work together to create a sensory experience that seeps into your bones and becomes a tactile memory you cannot easily forget.

Slowing down to write a letter while holding a sleek new pen in hand can be a joyful moment, and there is satisfaction in seeing the inky trail of words left behind on the paper. A fascinating dance happens between the head, the hand, and the pen nib. The pen moves and sways over the paper while something beautiful emerges.

Paper, pen, and ink have served us well for thousands of years. Next time you sit down to write a letter, stop for a moment and pay homage to all they have done for humankind. Now, write with abandon. And know that it is because of this wonderful, artful tool that posterity will have a record of.

The Postmark/Stamp Cancel

Stamp cancellation marks on letters and postcards serve as a testimonial to each letter's unique travel experience between sender and recipient.

It's all in the details.

Who would have imagined that a stamped letter and an odd configuration of ink splotches and curvy lines could ignite a lifelong passion and hobby in so many people? Without the letter, philately, the hobby of collecting stamps and their related cancellations and postmarks would not exist.

There's a Collector for Everything

My mother loved the little details of life: the care and the craftmanship someone invested in making something unique or beautiful, the human history that items represented. In her eyes, an intricately carved spoon or candle box was as much a piece of fine art as a painting in an art gallery.

Because my mother was a collector herself, she understood the minds of other collectors—individuals who become fixated on odd bits and relics of our past, things like old medical devices, glass insulators for telephone poles, butter churns, old wooden thread spools, comic books, chamber pots, breadboards . . . almost anything you can imagine. Finding and buying the objects of their desire makes collectors very, very happy people. It is hard to argue with happy.

Later in life, my mother became an antiques dealer. She would regularly answer ads in the newspapers placed by families who were getting rid of things—all kinds of things. Our dining room table at home would often hold the spoils of her searches. Sometimes, I was surprised and confused by the things she bought for resale. "Mom," I would say, holding up something from the table. "Really? Do people actually collect this junk?"

"Oh yes!" she would say. "You'd be surprised, Lynne. There is a collector for *everything*." As I watched some of these "odd" things sell quickly, I began to see what she meant. The beauty of a hobby or collection is in the eye of the beholder, so she taught me not to judge.

It was no surprise to me, then, as I researched this book, to find out that there are people who passionately collect not only postage stamps but also the inky, wavy, or pictorial postmarks that cancel postage stamps.

To most of us, the postmark is an afterthought at best. We might see an inky blotch or smeared date and place of origin in black ink on the front right quadrant of our letters and be completely nonplussed. To a collector, however, the postmark is a thing of beauty.

Stamp cancellations and postmarks are important to the history of the letter for several reasons. First, they are the proof that an old stamp is authentic, since it is difficult to forge a postmark on stamps. Second, the postmark serves as a time marker; it tells us exactly when a letter was posted. This can be valuable if the letter inside the envelope did not include the date it was written.

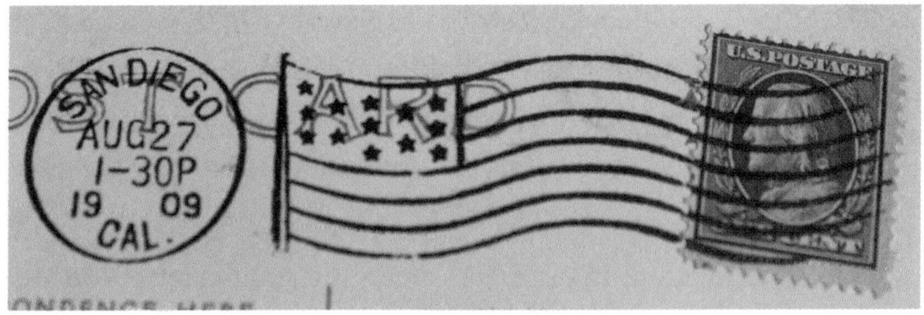

An example of a postmark and stamp cancel.

A postmark can also help the recipient of a letter calculate the time it took for the piece of mail to make its way to their mailbox. Recently, I have received postcards from Russia, Finland, Germany, Ireland, Belarus, Hong Kong, and Norway, all postmarked between three to four weeks before arriving at my home. Because I am part of a postcard exchange club, I take note of the amount of time it takes for each postcard to reach my home. For me, the waiting only increases feelings of excitement as I anticipate their arrival at my home.

There are usually two kinds of inscriptions on a mailed letter: a stamp cancel and a postmark. A stamp cancel is the mark used to deface or "cancel" a postage stamp and prevent its unlawful reuse. These are often referred to as an "obliterator" or "killer" marks.[139] Postmarks document where and when a piece of mail was posted. In some cases, a postal marking can also serve as a stamp cancel. Thus, the terms *stamp cancel* and *postmark* are used interchangeably.[140]

The postmark collector typically specializes in collecting certain kinds of postmarks:[141]

- **Discontinued Post Office Cancels.** Some towns have lost their post offices for some reason. The shorter the time that the post office operated in a specific town and the smaller the population it served, the greater the value of the postmark.
- **Rail Post Office (RPO) Cancels.** In earlier times, railroads attached a post office car to a train. Postal clerks would cancel and sort the mail as the train carried them from town to town.

- **Trolley Post Office Cancels.** Several cities (Chicago, Rochester, St. Louis, Boston, Brooklyn, Baltimore) used trolleys to pick up, cancel, and sort mail. The trolley serviced mailboxes along their specific routes and had all remaining mail sorted by the time they reached the main post office.
- **RFD Cancels.** A mail carrier made the stamp cancels on top of the stamps as they moved along on a postal route. The letter or packages were delivered to the recipient on the same postal route on the same day.
- **Places.** The collector may focus on collecting postmarks within a certain geographic area (states, counties, etc.). Some people collect the postmark from every post office in their state.[142]
- **Famous Names/Slogans.** Some people seek postmarks that include the names of famous people (think baseball players and advertising slogans).[143]
- **Cities and Towns with the Names of Presidents.** This might include postmarks from cities like Lincoln, Nebraska; Clinton, Iowa; Truman, Wisconsin, for examples.
- **Times of Historic Pandemics.** Some people even collect postmarks with evidence of having been disinfected by the postal service during previous pandemics, such as scorch marks, perforations, stains, and incisions, as well as the distinctive cancellations used to mark mail as "treated."[144]

Please consider sharing your old, unwanted postcards and letters with eager postmark collectors. They might find something in your cache that has eluded them for years and would round out their prized collection, giving them a thrill only an avid collector can experience.

The Postcard: A Simple Feast for the Eyes

The postcard—a diminutive greeting, a tantalizing visual delight. The history of the postcard is more complex than you would imagine. It took many years for it to evolve to be the postcard we recognize today. The history of the postcard in the United States began immediately before the Civil War period.[145] At first, postcards were strictly utilitarian tools for communicating—and low on aesthetic appeal. Much later, they would become the four-color beauties we have grown to love and collect.

In 1861, the United States Congress created a law that allowed for the use of privately printed cards, weighing one ounce or less, to be sent through the mail. Later that year, John P. Charlton from Philadelphia patented a postal card and sold the rights to Hymen Lipman, founder of the first envelope company in the United States and inventor of the lead pencil and eraser.[146] However, with the start of the Civil War a month later, Lipman Cards, as they were known, were largely forgotten and not seen again for nearly a decade. Lipman Cards finally began circulating in October 1870, becoming the first postcards mailed in the United States.[147]

The US Congress passed legislation on June 8, 1872, that approved government production of postal cards. The first government-produced postcard was issued on May 1, 1873. The new law allowed for only government-issued postcards to be manufactured and called *Postal Cards*.[148]

The US government later allowed private companies to print souvenir picture postcards in the early 1890s. In 1893, the first picture postcard was printed to commemorate the World's Columbian Exposition in Chicago.[149] In 1901, the words *Post Card* could be printed on the back of privately printed postcards.[150] By 1907, the US Postal Congress decreed that the public may only write personal messages on the left side of the address side of the postcard. This move created a significant shift in the postcard industry, which some have called the "divided back period," which spans 1907–1915.[151] During this period, "real photo postcards" were first produced from Kodak camera images.[152]

In the United States, a love affair with the postcard began in earnest during the years 1908–1913.[153] In fact, postcard collecting became such a fad that nearly one billion postcards were mailed in the United States in 1913 alone.[154] Collectors carefully placed their postcards in albums so that friends and families could ooh and aah over them at social gatherings. Chromolithographic printing with its rich, royal hues did lend charm and beauty to the postcards of that period, and I can understand why people are still inspired to collect them.

An example of the beauty and charm of chromolithographic printing on early postcards.

Old postcards from the turn of the twentieth century sometimes carry endearing or amusing messages—reflections of times when people had fewer expectations and more limited life experiences. For example,

> December 29, 1908
>
> Dear Father:
>
> How are you? I hope you are all well. I am a great deal better. I can raise my head now. But my ear still bothers me. We are having a dull and rainy day here. I wish you all a Happy New Year. Love to you all—Lillie

Postcards were often addressed in a rather cryptic fashion, sometimes using only the recipient's first and last name and the town and state where that person lived. Regardless, they were successfully delivered—probably because in many cases, the postmen knew everyone in town.

After World War I, postcards became increasingly sophisticated and visually appealing, with the advent of white border, linen, photochrome, and holographic cards. Sadly, the golden age of postcards appears to be behind us, but the souvenir postcard industry has managed to hold on by a thread. According to reporters at Market Watch, an online financial news service, England's oldest postcard publisher, J. Salmon, which had produced picturesque cards since 1890, ceased publication of its postcards in 2018. It should not surprise us to see postcard companies like J. Salmon closing up shop. Just twenty-five years ago, more than twenty million postcards were sold each year. That number has fallen to five or six million in recent years.[155]

While this saddens me, it is encouraging to know that there are many people who still enjoy sending and receiving postcards the old-fashioned way. Others continue to collect and trade them, a hobby called *deltiology*. Some postcards can be worth a great deal, especially if a valuable stamp is affixed to them.

Today, I rarely travel anywhere without sending at least a few postcards to friends or family back home. My hope is to prop up a sagging industry and ensure that postcards continue to be available for years to come.

Snail Mail Gloriously Lives on for Some Postcard Enthusiasts

Recently, I discovered an online association called Postcrossing. The goal of this organization is to facilitate the exchange of postcards between its members who are located all over the world. Members find joy in sending and receiving cards with people from different countries, cultures, interests, and backgrounds—much as they did more than one hundred years ago when international postal exchanges were popular. I was intrigued by this idea and so joined for free. For every postcard I send to a random name, I receive one in return from another randomly selected postcard enthusiast living somewhere in the world. On the back of the postcard might be a one-line greeting or something more, including poems, stamps, the sender's background and interests, or simple kind wishes.

Participating in this fun hobby encourages you to think of yourself as a citizen of the world, where formal boundaries don't necessarily matter much. You never know where the next visually appealing card and message will come from. The diversity of Postcrossing's membership keeps me curious about the world I live in and happy to be connected to interesting souls living far from me. Through the exchange of postcards and messages, we find that we have more in common than we might imagine. What better step toward world peace than to exchange a bit of beauty and kindness with such a diverse group of neighbors?

Postcards are a simple and sweet gift under any circumstances—whether they travel to your friends, family members, neighbors, coworkers, or total strangers. Next time you are traveling and sight-seeing, please go into the nearest souvenir shop and find an interesting, oddly humorous, or beautiful postcard. Write a charming message for the recipient. No bragging allowed. Include the iconic phrase *Wish you were here* and imagine their face when they open their mailbox and find your lovely card there to greet them. No matter how technology-driven that person may be, I guarantee you will be creating happiness. In sending your postcard, you might also provide inspiration for their next travel adventure. And with patience, you may just receive a card in return.

A Letter to the Bridegroom's Oak

"Mighty oaks from little acorns grow" is a common old saying that means that out of something small or inconsequential, great things may grow to be something significant or surprising. Like acorns, new love nurtured and supported will grow to sustain and inspire those committed to it. And what better way to grow a new relationship than to write the always-cherished love letter to the object of one's affections?

We have discussed the impact of the love letter and its important role in creating intimacy and affection between two people. Most of us take for granted that the US Postal Service does an efficient and dependable job of delivering love messages to our sweethearts. But what happens when two people must keep their love a secret and leave no obvious physical evidence of their forbidden union? In these circumstances, you must find creative new ways of exchanging intimate messages.

Such was the case when two people fell in love in the Dodauer Forest in Germany in the late 1800s. Because at first their relationship was not approved of, they could not be seen together nor share their love in any public way. Instead, they turned to Mother Nature to assist them in continuing their relationship in secret.

So once upon a time (1890, to be exact), in Bräutigamseiche at Eutin, in the state of Schleswig-Holstein in Germany, the son of a chocolate maker, Herr Schütte-Felsche, and the daughter of a forester, Fräulein Ohrt, met and fell in love. The union unfortunately did not meet the approval of the young woman's father, so he forbade her from continuing the relationship. Careful to stay out of the public eye and the critical eye of the young woman's father, they began to secretly leave love letters to one another in a hole in the trunk of an old oak tree located in town.[156]

Legend has it that by and by, the father of the young woman became aware of their secret relationship and their strong devotion to one another. Over time, his views of the relationship softened, and on June 2, 1891, he allowed their marriage to go forward, holding them a large wedding reception beneath the branches of the great old oak where their love affair blossomed.

Word began to spread about the old tree, and some people began believing that the tree had the magical powers to matchmake lonely souls. Consequently, thousands of people wrote letters to the tree in hopes that it would create the same magic for them as it had for the two young lovers.[157]

By 1927, so many letters began arriving at the Eutin post office that the German postal service (Deutsche Bundespost) made an audacious decision to give the tree a proper address:

Bräutigamseiche
Dodauer Forest
23701 Eutin, Germany

The German postal service also provided an easy way to access the tree's letter hole by erecting a sturdy ten-foot ladder for those visiting the tree in person. While standing on the ladder, visitors can read through the love letters already deposited in the tree's trunk or leave a love letter of their own for someone else to read. The only "rule" is that if you open and read a letter and decide you are not interested in answering it, you must put it back so the next visitor can find and enjoy it.[158]

In addition to serving as a depository for love letters, the tree is believed to be a lucky charm for those who are already in love. Young women believe that if they walk around the base of the tree three times during a full moon while thinking of their beloved, they will be married within the year.

Now, you might have concerns about anyone who would put their trust in a tree's ability to connect lonely hearts. But for more than one hundred years, the Bridegroom's Oak has regularly performed its magic, reportedly resulting in the marriage of some hundred or more couples. That averages around one marriage a year. It is hard to argue with results like that.

Today, the five-hundred-year-old, eighty-two-foot oak tree still stands, having been designated as a "tree of national significance." The tree was the soil, the letters were the seeds. Human longing and belief were the sun and water. The love that grows is surely sweet.

The Bridegroom's Oak tree, still in its glory.

Sending Letters to a Neighborhood Elf

Children connect with nature and their own imaginations far easier than most of the rest of us. It is no wonder, then, that they can see fairies dancing amid garden greenery, overhear trees talking in the woods, and communicate with elves and brownies in their secret gardens. In fact, children have been communicating with one neighborhood elf in Minneapolis, Minnesota, for more than twenty-five years.

Children come by the hundreds with parents in tow, hoping to see his very tiny home just off the walking path that encircles Lake Harriet and down the road from the rose garden, located in the trunk of a tree. His name is Mr. Little Guy. According to local legend, Mr. Little Guy was born in the 1200s and now resides on the lakeshore from Memorial Day to Labor Day each year, along with his wife, Martha, a daughter, Alta Lucia, and a cat named Whizzbang.[159]

Children regularly write letters to Mr. Little Guy, or Thom as his friends call him. They leave their letters, candy, trinkets, and toys

Mr. Little Guy's home on Lake Harriet in Minneapolis, Minnesota —a popular place for children to visit.

behind his tiny, ornate front door, the one with the brass knocker and fancy hinges.

No one has ever actually seen Mr. Little Guy, but he exists in the hearts and minds of thousands of children—especially those who have received his return letters, which are written on tiny silver cards, in very tiny type. "Dear Gillian, Sonia, Kate and Elizabeth," he writes. "Thank you for the stickers. They were so nice I have put them up in my bedroom and look at them every night before I go to bed. This is my cabin. My real home is farther away . . . You have to be really sharp to see me."[160]

Mr. Little Guy is only about six inches tall, he tells us. He and his family are particularly fond of samba, minnow cakes, and pizza. He drives a mini-minivan. He gives credit to ladybugs for his jokes, complains about being harassed by neighborhood squirrels and chipmunks, and feels a lack of respect from local woodchucks.[161]

The Big People (humans) have made it hard for Mr. Little Guy to live in peace. Mr. Little Guy's cabin has been vandalized several times, and the magical elf's patience does have its limits. Once, he left this letter for the neighborhood bullies tormenting him: "Life is good, but I have to tell you I am getting a little discouraged with the Big People. Our cottage is being visited with an undue portion of hostility this summer. Someone keeps taking the darn door. So far this summer, the landlord has had to replace the door nine times and he is not happy."[162]

Despite the struggles, this elusive elf continues his work of answering between fifteen hundred and two thousand letters each summer. It takes a lot of effort, he confesses, but the work is important. He writes responses to the letters he receives whenever he can—early in the day, late in the day, and in his spare time.[163] Mr. Little Guy is all about leaving a legacy in his community. He wants us to know: "Elves by nature try to leave a legacy. Some work for Santa Claus and put up with his demanding hours and rather cold working conditions. Others, like the Keeblers, make an outstanding cookie even though they appear in those ridiculous TV commercials. Trust me, those cartoons on screen no more look like a real elf than you do."[164]

In addition to receiving sweet and charming letters, sometimes Mr. Little Guy reads especially heartbreaking news. He has been known to cry at times. "It's the kids with cancer that write and it's adults with cancer, and it's adults that have never found love and adults that have lost love," he reveals.[165] His main goal is to let people know they are not alone.

Looking into the future, you can envision many adults passing along their stories of the magical tree, a benevolent elf, and the letter that made them believe in magic—and even in themselves. For, like many letters we cherish, Mr. Little Guy is always sure to include an important message at the end of every letter he writes: "I believe in you."

And because of his letters, we, in return, believe in him, too.

The Subtle, Loving Language of . . . a Postage Stamp?

As I observe the world of pop culture, my senses often feel overwhelmed, sometimes assaulted. For an artist to be seen or heard, the shocking or outrageous must continually be ramped up to the point where it can grow tedious, tiresome, or offensive to the observer.

I realize that there are times when we need to be shocked out of our complacency, so the arts and media have a role to play in ensuring this happens. However, we also need the healing balm of loving images and content—things that celebrate the goodness in us and the world around us.

When I need healing, I purposely seek out nature, music, or the arts, knowing that any or all will lift me up. I also look for pure expressions of the heart as the antidote to the mean and hurtful things I see around me. Oftentimes, the letter-writing process is the antidote for all that seems too fast, too chaotic, or harmful in the world.

I like this space.

During the Victorian era, well-heeled people in England found their own subtle ways of coping with the world they lived in. One way was to create a unique way of expressing their love that I find particularly charming. English society at the time was not known for encouraging the expression of personal sentiments and emotion. So people crafted secret "languages" that delivered coded messages to those they most admired.

Well-to-do Victorians in particular had the leisure time and privilege to popularize certain hobbies and pastimes devoted to courtship, friendship, and romance, including the language of flowers and the language of postage stamps.

The language of postage stamps? Yes, indeed. The language of postage stamps was the means to express forbidden love, display affection for friends and relatives, or convey longing for a romantic interest.

The language of stamps provided a secret way to communicate with your beloved during Victorian times.

In those times, keeping a stiff upper lip and keeping your feelings to yourself were proper behaviors among polite society. Unfortunately, this made expressing your true emotions about anything meaningful all the more difficult. The language of stamps made certain kinds of communication easier. This "illicit" stamp code also provided a way for young lovers to convey secret love messages to one another, escaping the prying eyes of nosey, disapproving parents who might stand in the way of their romance.

Flowers and postage stamps took the place of the words people longed to say but could not.

Mastering these new languages took some study. You had to be careful not to send the wrong secret message to your beloved or make a faux pas that might cause embarrassment. For example, how you affixed the stamp to the envelope conveyed a coded message. So if you wanted to tell someone that you loved them, you would place the stamp upside down on the envelope's upper-left corner.

Here are some other options for sending a secret message:[166]

- Upside down, top-left corner = I love you
- Upside down, top-right corner = Write no more
- Crosswise, top-left corner = My heart is another's
- Center of envelope, at top = Yes
- Center of envelope, at bottom = No
- Straight up and down, any position = Good-bye, sweetheart
- At right angle, top-right corner = Do you love me?
- At right angle, top-left corner = I hate you
- Upright, top-right corner = I desire your friendship
- Upright, in line with surname = Accept my love
- Upside down, in line with surname = I am engaged
- At right angle, in line with the surname = I long to see you
- Centered, right edge = Write immediately!

To understand the real intentions of their admirers, Victorians had to have a floral dictionary and a postage stamp decoder to decipher the meanings of these silent messages.

Sending codes and messages using stamps is believed to have begun during the Austro-Hungarian Empire in the 1860s. The English popularized the practice in the 1880s, and it quickly spread across Europe and other countries around the world. The peak in popularity for the language of stamps was during Victorian times (late 1800s–early 1900s).[167]

The stamp code encouraged irregular and inconsistent stamp placement on envelopes, which became challenging for postal services across the globe. When letters and postcards were still hand-stamped, it did not matter as much where the stamp was placed on the envelope. However, with the advent of high-speed canceling machines, the consistency and efficiency of the approach became more important.[168]

Out of necessity, postal services from around the world worked together to create new postal regulations that required all mail to have its stamps affixed within the upper right-hand corner of a letter or postcard.[169] It is believed that this position was selected to coincide with the dominant right-handedness of most mail handlers.[170]

Yes, the new postal regulations made things tidy and predictable, all right, but who knows how much anxiety they caused when this secret language was taken from proper gentlemen, genteel young ladies, or others not terribly good with their words. Today, a few people might still cling to a modified postage stamp code to send covert messages of love. The upside-down stamp still conveys "I love you," for example.

The good news is that people are adaptable and more able to express their feelings in more adult ways. Thankfully, love has continued to flourish even without the rather clumsy and obtuse language of stamps.

The Bird-Brained Letter Carrier

When I hear the rumbling *thunk, thunk* of footsteps on our front porch, I know that 90 percent of the time, it is our postal carrier delivering the mail. It's a comforting sound. Theirs is a job most of us wouldn't want to do and probably take for granted. On the bitterly cold or horribly humid days, I feel great appreciation for the hard work they do for me. Without them, I would never have had the wonderful letter-writing experiences I've had and most certainly would not be writing this book. To all of them, I tip my hat.

Delivering our mail, day in and day out, takes a serious team effort. Many individuals must coordinate their efforts so that we receive our letters and our packages arrive on time in all kinds of weather. These synchronized activities ensure that the wheels of commerce continue to turn and people around the world receive important personal correspondence. There is, however, one member of that team who has never gotten the recognition and appreciation they deserved. It's time we become more acquainted with their heroic contributions to postal history.

Welcome to the world of the pigeon post. Now largely a thing of the past, the pigeon post involves using homing pigeons to deliver short messages to people many miles away, under circumstances where traditional methods of communication are impossible or ineffective.[171] Pigeons have a remarkable homing instinct that allows them to be taken to a location far from their home, to have a message fastened to their bodies (usually using a metal tube strapped to a leg), then allowed to fly home with their message reliably in tow.[172]

The pigeon post relies on a specific variety of domestic pigeon (*Columba livia domestica*), which was derived from the wild rock dove and selectively bred over hundreds of years for its ability to dependably find its way home over extremely long distances and difficult conditions.[173]

The pigeon's partnership with human beings has been a long and celebrated one. Scholars believe that people have been domesticating pigeons for over five thousand years.[174] The earliest historical reference to pigeons being used to carry messages between people dates to 2500 BCE. By the 1100s, people were regularly using pigeons to deliver messages between the Middle East, Europe, and India.[175] By the late 1800s, pigeons were used commercially by banks and news services in Europe to share information quickly and inexpensively.[176]

During the late 1800s and early 1900s, military commanders also relied on pigeons to convey top secret orders and warnings during wartime. Here, the birds were commonly known as *war pigeons*.[177] Their ability to securely—and rather dependably—transmit top secret information across long distances made them useful during the Franco-Prussian War (1870–71).[178] Pigeons continued to play a strategic military role as late as World Wars I and II.[179]

During World War I, one pigeon was duly recognized by the French government for his honorable service, receiving the Croix de Guerre medal, a military decoration normally given to soldiers for their great valor. Named Cher Ami, the pigeon suffered multiple gunshot wounds in the battlefield but continued to meet his objective, delivering a message that saved the surviving members of the Lost Battalion.[180]

During the same war, the British Intelligence Service used pigeons to maintain contact with sympathizers and resistance movements in enemy-occupied territory. Sometimes, batches of pigeons, each with its own body harness and parachute, were ejected from airplanes at regular intervals by a clockwork mechanism. Many died upon landing; however, on several occasions, the pigeons were able to return to their roosts with essential messages despite bad weather, bullets, and natural predators.[181]

We owe our bird friends a great deal. Without them, history might read differently today. Pigeons' ability to get through dangerous or difficult circumstances when humans couldn't made them ideal partners and allies in human history. During peacetime, they have been efficient and effective messengers for medicine and personal correspondence, moving unfettered at a remarkable speed of up to sixty miles an hour and nearly a thousand miles in two days.[182]

At present, enthusiasts still train and race pigeons, keeping this ancient tradition alive. In fact, it is still possible to have a letter delivered by pigeon post to your favorite pen pal or loved one. The next time you want to find a surefire way to deliver your special love letter, call on your reliable, amiable, and often misunderstood birdbrained postal carrier to save the day.

W. Reginald Bray: The Human Letter

We all know people who have taken a hobby or interest to the point of obsession. Their hobby might involve collecting matchbooks or wristwatches, buying old radios, gardening, birding, or running marathons. The *Oxford Dictionary* defines an obsession as "an idea or thought that continually preoccupies or intrudes on a person's mind." Note that this definition does not make any judgments about whether an obsession is a positive or negative thing.

Among postal enthusiasts, one man proved that having an obsession can be a good thing. Having an unwavering focus on one interest, and a consistent practice, allowed him to satisfy his own curiosity and create an unusual postal legacy in the process. Whether it was collecting signatures on postcards from famous people or sending a turnip through the mail, this man managed to take his rather peculiar interest in England's postal system to a very high level indeed.

Our man, Mr. W. Reginald Bray (1879–1939), became obsessed with Britain's Royal Mail system and seemed to delight in confounding local postal workers and regularly testing their patience. Given the number of pranks and challenges he came up with over many years, I imagine that he must have spent a good many of his waking hours dreaming up the next out-of-the-box postal "experiment."

Specifically, Bray wanted to see how far he could challenge what the postal service would accept as a "letter" or "post" and test whether they would deliver them to the correct addresses.

In his entertaining biography *The Englishman Who Posted Himself and Other Curious Objects*, author John Tingey chronicles Bray's lifelong obsession with postal curiosities and his desire to become the autograph king of his day.

Bray was born in 1879 to a middle-class family in Forest Hill, England. His obsession with the mail began with a childhood passion for collecting stamps and postmarks.[183] In 1898, Bray decided to purchase the official *Post Office Guide* for the Royal Mail.[184] Apparently, the way in which postal customers had to address letters, as well as the Royal Mail's responsibilities for delivering them, captured the attention of the young man. How far could he go in testing the postal service's willingness to adhere to their own rules—specifically the one requiring that "all letters have to be delivered as addressed"?[185]

Over the years, Bray created all sorts of what he called "freak letters" to test the postal system, including addressing and mailing a frying pan, a bowler hat, a bicycle pump, a starched shirt cuff, seaweed, a flask, and even a rabbit's skull in the daily mail.[186] In most cases, the Royal Mail delivered the "letters" as promised, but Bray was not always successful in his attempts, and some "letters" or postcards were returned to him.

Bray was also intrigued with that portion of the postal code that stated that citizens could post anything—even living creatures as small as a bee to one the size of an elephant.[187] This promise presumably got his creative juices flowing, concluding with his audacious and successful attempt to send both his dog and himself through the mail. He prided himself on being the first "human letter" to be delivered by the Royal Mail via registered post.[188]

W. Reginald Bray's audacious and successful attempt to have himself delivered to his father's home.

Some of Bray's other antics involved trying to stump the mail carriers who sorted and delivered the mail. For example, he addressed a postcard by writing backward, embedded the destination for a postcard in a rhyme, and wrote an address in the form of a riddle.[189]

You have to wonder how the postal officials reacted to all of it. He did become somewhat of a celebrity in England for his peculiar activities, so most postal workers seem to have taken it all in stride. One postman, however, got even. Having a bit of fun himself, he returned one of Bray's postcards to him and added his own amusing rhyme to the front of the card.[190]

In his later years, Bray explained what caused him to embark on this unusual postal pastime in the first place:

> Some time ago, it occurred to me to venture on the post office authorities, several letters, in both form and address. This course I did not enter upon without much consideration and hesitancy, for it would be most unfair, to say the least of it, to cause a lot of unnecessary trouble, merely for the sake of playing a senseless prank. My object from the beginning was to test the ingenuity of the postal authorities, and if possible, to vindicate them of the charges of "carelessness and neglect. Should these lines come before the eyes of any official through whose hands my "trick letters" have passed, I hope he will accept this explanation as an apology for any extra trouble that I may have caused him."[191]

Bray's fascination with the postal system lasted for more than forty years.[192] Tingey credits Bray for being one of the first pioneers of mail art. Without a doubt, his many postal experiments did showcase his innate cleverness and creativity. English society of his time did take note. He became a sought-after writer, speaker, and exhibitor about mail curiosities.[193]

Over his lifetime, Bray collected many thousands of postal items, which his wife and daughtered inherited when he died in 1939. Most of the vast collection was sold by his heirs to one collector in the 1950s. The fate of that collection is not known; however, some collectors believe that it has likely been split up and sold off to other collectors.[194]

Bray surrounded by the spoils of his lifelong obsession.

Bray, like so many hobbyists, must have spent untold hours focused on this one rather peculiar interest. Yet his pioneering work continues to bring amusement to others who enjoy letters and mail-related hobbies. I, for one, appreciate his impish originality and zest for life. Because of people like W. Reginald Bray, letters and cards continue to surprise, engage, and entertain us in ever-changing ways, sustaining their allure for all time.

Letters Lost and Found

I think there is a bit of a treasure hunter in all of us. Who hasn't dreamed of striking it rich purely by accident? Some of us have been lucky enough to find money or a lost ring in a parking lot, on a beach, down a couch, or in the street.

We have all seen or heard stories of individuals who found remarkable treasures in dumpsters, in farm fields, underneath the floorboards, and in the walls of old homes. Is it any surprise, then, that people find it exciting when they discover old, dirty, crusty bottles washed up on beaches? What could be more thrilling than finding out that they contain a fragile, old letter from someone who is no longer alive or who lives halfway around the world?

A letter in a bottle combines the excitement of finding lost treasure with the thrill of collecting a piece of human history. Historians believe that people have been sending messages in bottles since at least 310 BCE, when the Greek philosopher Theophrastus used the tactic to test ocean currents. These "drift bottles" are still in use today by scientists who research ocean currents.[195]

Beyond conducting scientific experiments, people have had many reasons for sending messages in bottles over the centuries. Some bottles have been tossed purely for fun, while others were thrown overboard to satisfy other pursuits. Here are a few of the stories of bottles lost and found:

1. **To Document a Historic Journey.** On his return trip from the New World, Christopher Columbus and his crew were caught in a serious storm at sea. Not certain that his ship or his crew would make it back to port in Spain, Columbus purportedly wrote an account of his "discovery," sealed it in a cask, and threw it into the sea. Along with the report was a request that whoever should find it should deliver it to the queen of Castile. No one has ever found this cask—or if they did, they did not report it.[196]

2. **Just for the Joy of It.** After 101 years, a grandfather's message in a bottle was delivered to his granddaughter. Angela Erdmann's grandfather had died six years before her birth. A century earlier, he placed a postcard in a sealed bottle, along with correct postage, and tossed it into the Baltic Sea. A hundred years passed until a fisherman caught the bottle in his fishing net and returned it to Angela to be read for the first time.[197]

3. **A Failed Attempt at Saving Lives.** In 1794, a Japanese seaman named Chunosuke Matsuyama and his forty-three fellow crewmen were shipwrecked on a South Pacific island. With no supplies to sustain them, all crew members died. Before they all expired, Matsuyama carved a message on a piece of coconut wood and put it inside a sealed bottle. It was not until 150 years later that their fate became known. The bottle eventually washed up near the Japanese village of Hiraturemura, Matsuyama's birthplace.[198]

4. **To Say Good-Bye.** A young Irishman, Jeremiah Burke, age nineteen, wrote his final good-bye on April 15, 1912. Burke, along with his cousin Nora Hegarty, were passengers on the ill-fated maiden voyage of the *Titanic*. Before the ship sank, Burke managed to write a brief note and had the presence of mind to find a bottle and seal the note inside before throwing it overboard. The note stated simply "From Titanic, good-bye all, Burke of Glanmire, Cork."[199]

5. **For Research.** The oldest *authenticated* letter in a bottle was discovered in 2018. The bottle had been thrown from a German ship in the Indian Ocean in 1886, later found by Tonya and Kym Illman on a remote beach on Wedge Island, Australia.[200]

   When the captain threw the bottle overboard, he stuffed a printed note inside that included the date, the ship's coordinates, the ship's name and captain, and the details of their departure and arrival in port for the purposes of oceanic research. The age of the bottle was later authenticated by the Federal Maritime and Hydrographic Agency of Germany and the Western Australian Museum.[201]

6. **For Philosophers.** In 2009, an Australian woman and her companion were sitting on the balcony of a cruise ship in Indonesia, pondering one of life's great questions: "Is it better to love or be loved?" She decided to write this question in a letter, put it in a bottle, and threw it overboard. They asked whoever found it to write to her and answer her question. The bottle traveled 5,600 miles to South Africa, where it was found more than a year later.

   The finder called the sender and gave her the following answer: "I found your bottle. It is better to be loved. But to be loved, you must love."[202]

Mailboxes That Spark Delight

Let's just say that not all of us have the same level of creative genius. I, for example, am more apt to be an observer than a creator. Fortunately for myself and others like me, there are creative souls out there who will allow us to come along on their daring, innovative, and inventive journeys. By witnessing their genius at play, we are encouraged—sometimes forced—to leave our comfort zones and experience something new, something challenging, maybe even joyful or whimsical. In this space, everything we might have taken for granted may be questioned, reimagined, redesigned, or repurposed.

Even the old conventions of letter writing and sending mail can be subject to rejuvenation and reinvention by creative people because artists are often perfectly comfortable rejecting the tried-and-true, customary ways of doing things. Thank goodness.

Take, for example, the old corner mailbox where we deposit our letters. I doubt very much that many of us see the mailbox as a place where human creativity can be unleashed or as a public art display. Well, think again, my friends.

In the United States, the basic, stodgy look of the curbside mailbox has not changed much for decades. When the federal government first designed curbside mail collection boxes, the lackluster green steel did little to enliven the senses. It appears that mailboxes were meant to serve as nothing more than a utilitarian repository to collect public mail. Sadly, in most of the United States, we've failed to see the pure potentiality of mailboxes as a place for creativity and fun. However, in other parts of the world, our global neighbors, even in remote parts of the world, have shattered convention and created some entertainment in the process.

Several other countries have decided to capitalize on their country's unique attractions and have created memorable snail mail experiences for tourists and other mail lovers. In fact, since their postal authorities threw caution to the wind, thousands of tourists have traveled to remote and unusual places just for the fun of mailing their letters and postcards:

1. Have you ever had the urge to mail your letter underwater? Not a problem! In May 2003, the Republic of Vanuatu, an island nation in the South Pacific Ocean, opened the first-ever underwater mailbox located under some nine feet of water within the Hideaway Island and Marine Sanctuary. Visitors who snorkel or dive can mail their waterproof postcards from the island's unusual, very soggy post office location. To ensure that the postmarks survive the saltwater environment, the postal service uses a unique embossing tool rather than traditional ink postmarks.[203]

   Other underwater mailboxes can be found in Susami Bay, Japan; Pulau Layang-Layang, Malaysia; and in Risør, Norway.[204]

2. The next time you feel the urge to climb the world's highest mountain and want your friends and neighbors

to hear about it, never fear. At the North Everest Base Camp, in Tibet, sits the highest post office in the world. However, to use this mailbox, you must first carry your letter to an elevation of 17,090 feet. It is not surprising that this post office experiences very light foot traffic each year.

3. The state of Michigan boasts the world's only floating post office aboard the *J. W. Westcott II.* This working post office has been in operation for 125 years, delivering mail to large ships on Lake Michigan.

4. In the bush on the Galápagos Islands, you can find another nonconforming mailbox concept. Among a pile of old barrels, crates, and boxes, there are postcards waiting to be picked up and sent through the mail. Visitors to the islands are invited to dig through the postcards to see if any are addressed to locations near their home. If visitors find one, islanders ask that they deliver it to the addressee themselves.[205]

5. In Japan, it is common to see public mailboxes made using whimsical designs—a fish, a decorative ginger jar, a miniature post office building, a stork[206]—on street corners. They add a bit of fun in urban environments. Why not make something beautiful or delightful instead of simply practical?

6. The Penguin Post Office, located on the Antarctic Peninsula, is the most popular tourist destination on the continent, not that it has much competition. This post office has a mailbox located at the farthest point south on planet Earth. The post office is operated by the United Kingdom's Heritage Trust. It is open only from November to May each year. The post office is mostly used by the residents of Port Lockroy;

> however, an additional eighteen thousand people each year (tourists who arrive here from cruise ships) also frequent the tiny office. Approximately seventy thousand of their postcards are sent from the Penguin Post Office to destinations around the globe each year.[207]

If we, too, see mailing letters and postcards as a fully sensory experience, we might discover creative ideas for reinventing mailboxes that are hiding in our towns and cities. Perhaps we could inspire more letter writing. Postage will never be free, but whimsy can be.

Writing the New and Preserving the Old

Encouraging the Next Generation of Letter Writers

We cannot love what we don't know. We cannot miss something we've never experienced. And there are literally millions of people in the world who have never known or experienced the joy of sending and receiving letters. If we want more people to step into the uncharted territory of all things postal, someone will need to show them the way. This is where leaders, mentors, and enthusiastic hobbyists come in—someone like you, perhaps.

For those souls who have never received anything other than junk mail in their mailboxes, we owe it to them to fill that void. We know that letters feed our hearts and minds, and I cannot think of a time in recent memory when people needed this kind of loving attention more. Can we get started soon? Yes, I say, please do!

We *Can* Model a New Old Way

It is probably no surprise that I have always tried to model the way and to spark an interest in letter writing in my own children. My efforts started early when my children were in elementary school. During those years, I received a gift catalog for children that sold, among other things, small metal mailbox banks. *How sweet,* I thought. *The kids would just love that.*

Well, one thing led to another, and I decided we needed to make a family post office through which we could send our "family mail." I envisioned that we would each have a post office box and "send" each other letters, love notes, Valentine's Day surprises, birthday greetings, and so on.

I enlisted the help of my handy father to make us the post office boxes. Each small cubbyhole had one of our names on it. Then I had to figure out an inexpensive way of creating a little post office building. I decided to use an old cardboard box to make our office. I cut away one side of the box so that we could access and see our post office from outside. I used some extra cardboard to construct a roof. I cut off the ends of wooden tongue depressors and overlapped them in rows to serve as a "tile" roof. Finally, I painted the whole structure, inside and out. Inside the post office, there was a desk, chair, scale for packages, desk accessories, mailbags, and our post office boxes. A small, stuffed bird was the postmaster. Outside, we placed our own diminutive mail collection box.

Every Valentine's Day, Easter, and Christmas, we made each other miniature cards and sent them through our little post office. This was a fun and cheap way to encourage giving, sharing, and letter writing. My kids loved our little post office, and so did I. Many years later, I disposed of the post office "building" but kept the remaining pieces in case I, or my children, want to re-create it in the future.

I still have the tiny cards and notes we exchanged with each other. Today, I am happy to report that my early efforts succeeded, as both my son and daughter write lovely thank-you notes and engaging letters to family members when they need or want to. I am hoping they will keep that tradition alive long after I am gone.

A Lost Art Rediscovered

A friend of mine is doing her part to keep letter writing alive for the next generation. Several years ago, she and her teenage nephew, Leo, began a pen pal relationship. She wasn't sure letter writing would hold her nephew's interest over time; however, once they got things in motion, neither wanted to stop.

The letters are anything but boring. The colorful stationeries and use of gel pens add vitality and joy to their words. And there is a

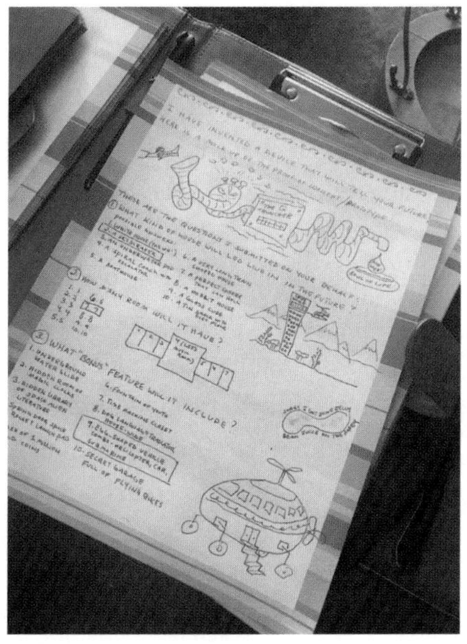

The delightful doodling on this handwritten letter makes it irresistible reading for any pen pal, young or old.

good deal of humor and whimsy in what they write to each other. My friend's letters include stories and writing prompts, accompanied by her fantastical, sometimes silly drawings that would delight anyone, young or old. Her wonderful sense of playfulness shines through, which he responds to in kind. These handmade beauties will likely be treasured for a lifetime and will have played a significant role in strengthening the bond between them.

She recently asked her nephew why he liked letter writing, an unusual hobby for someone his age. He responded, "I like letters because you get to hold the same paper that the letter writer held when he or she wrote it. It is sort of like a long-distance handshake or hug. It also allows you to practice your handwriting."

How very lucky these two are to have each other in their lives!

Reciprocity Between the Generations

My aunt's husband, Wayne, no longer with us, also regularly wrote letters to his grandchildren—all now adults—even though some lived quite close to him. He described their exchanges in very positive ways and with a twinkle in his eye. His grandchildren were also enthusiastic about writing him in return.

A millennial professional recently said to me, "I love letters, but no one ever sends me any." *How sad*, I thought. I almost volunteered to become her pen pal to fill the void.

Fortunately, there are other people also keeping this art form alive. Like those dedicated to preserving blacksmithing, candle making, stone carving, lace making, and so on, we can ensure that handwritten letters never vanish from our culture. One woman refused to let go of handwritten letters as a means of communication, despite her common use of multiple social media platforms. Her name is Dinah Johnson, and she has created an online club for letter writers, called the Handwritten Letter Appreciation Society. Now over seven hundred members strong, she continues to inspire people to keep this age-old practice alive. Bless her.

Letter Writing in a Sea of Distractions

Gardening is both a happy obsession and a dreaded responsibility, depending on the day that you ask me about my favorite hobby. I start each year with the greatest of intentions. It begins in midwinter. You will often see me gushing over the pages of garden catalogs, magazines, or books, dreaming of the ways in which this year's garden will be better than last year's—this time with a more nuanced blend of color, composition, and texture, a better home for birds and bees.

Later, when the snow goes out, I cannot wait to get into the flower beds: clearing, trimming, planting, repositioning, and mulching. It is the most gratifying feeling to be part of nature's dependable and miraculous cycles and rhythms. But then, before I know what happened, the dog days of summer come along, and my initial enthusiasm begins to wane. In fact, there is a negative correlation between the growth of creeping Charlie and my level of enthusiasm, and between the increasing heat and my sense of earthly duties. It is this time of the summer that I must dig deep to find inspiration and discipline so that my garden survives another year and can greet me again next spring.

Making Time for the Things We Love

A good way to have a more balanced, less stressful life is to take up a relaxing hobby or to pursue a special interest you find challenging, yet purely enjoyable. For some, this might mean collecting things you love, like stamps, books, antique tools, vintage jewelry, or vinyl records. Some might find it rewarding and fulfilling to spend free time in the service of others. And then there are those who want to relax by making things with their hands, creating three-dimensional objects that will last, like furniture, paintings, toys, sculptures, quilts, or handwritten letters. But how can we start something new in our lives or sustain the old when we are already so distracted, overwhelmed, or busy doing other important things?

When it comes to establishing and sustaining a new hobby or leisure activity, some are probably easier than others. Letter writing seems much more doable, for example, than running marathons, building a desk, or making a canoe by hand. It requires few tools or special materials. Nevertheless, time, or our perception of it, becomes the most important barrier. Even when we embrace a simpler hobby, procrastination can get the better of us. I know. There were times in the middle of my life, as I was immersed in a career and raising a family, when writing a four-page letter seemed like climbing Mount Everest. My discipline was nil even though my enthusiasm never wavered.

Hobbies Are Difficult to Start and Sustain—Or Are They?

Many people tell me that they do not have the time to write letters, do not know how to make the time, or simply would rather take the easier way out to text or email when it comes to communicating with someone else. I understand this. We're very rational beings when it comes to conserving energy and taking the path of least resistance. We will take the easy way out nine times out of ten—and that is okay. But perhaps we should put that tenth time aside to invest ourselves in something we would find truly meaningful and soulful.

Letter writing is one activity that I try to make time for, because letters are such an important way to connect with people I care about. I am convinced of this, because so many people have gone out of their way to thank me for my letters, as humble and ordinary as they are. My loved ones are worth that bit of extra effort—the special stationery I find for them, the carefully chosen stamps I affix to their envelopes.

If you find the idea of letter writing appealing, there might be a way to set reasonable expectations for yourself, without adding unnecessary stress to your life in the process.

The End of Procrastination?

If you tend to procrastinate when a task is new or perceived to be difficult, you are certainly not alone. Letter writing can seem like a huge hurdle to clear, even though you might deeply care about a person and can imagine how happy they would be to read your clever and entertaining words. Overwhelmed by the task, you might freeze up. Suddenly, you would rather clean the cat box than take out pen and paper. Not surprisingly, that letter never gets written.

In his book *Atomic Habits*, author James Clear discusses why new habits are often difficult to start and to stick to, and how we can overcome the odds of failing at something that we really want to do. He writes on his own website, "Too often, we let our motivations and desires drive us into a frenzy as we try to solve our entire problem at once, instead of starting a small, new routine . . . . If you are serious about making real change—in other words, if you're serious about doing things better than you are now—then you have to start small."[208]

Clear asks us to begin by making tiny changes in our habits so that the brain can adjust to learning something new and then, when it becomes more routine, to easily repeat it. Often, he says, we sabotage ourselves by setting our goals too high and creating too many conditions for achieving them: *I must use gorgeous stationery, practice my cursive writing first, write at least a six-page letter*, and so on. Setting realistic, achievable goals is an important first step.[209]

Early in the process, Clear suggests that you get into the right mindset about the new habit (e.g., letter writing) you want to consistently practice. Rather than seeing the new habit as something you *have to do*, you can take a different tack and say to yourself instead, "Wow! Today, I am so lucky to have the time to write a letter to my dear friend Katherine!" Seeing your new habit as an opportunity rather than as a burden helps you to get things off to a good start and increases the likelihood of long-term success.[210]

Clear has developed an easy strategy for successfully initiating and then continuing to practice a new hobby or activity you care about. He calls it the Two-Minute Rule.[211] The Two-Minute Rule involves taking a significant goal you have set for yourself, and then dividing this new goal into small, bite-size tasks that anyone would be able to accomplish in two minutes or less. This prevents you from feeling overwhelmed by the enormity of the larger goal. Being able to set small goals and then reach them builds your sense of achievement and feelings of self-mastery. Before you know it, you have reached your larger, more challenging goal.[212]

Here, I take a shot at applying Clear's Two-Minute Rule to letter writing to demonstrate how you could break the activity down into bite-size nuggets that feel very manageable in a hectic world:

> Day 1: Select your paper (nice stationery or whatever you have handy), a writing instrument, and envelope. Leave them out on your desk ready for the next day.
>
> Day 2: Locate your address book or smartphone and put the recipient's address on the envelope. Add a simple flourish to

the envelope or letter—perhaps a sketch, a beautiful stamp, a lovely sticker, and so on.

Day 3: Write the first page of your letter. Congratulate yourself for having gotten this far.

Day 4: Continue the letter until it is finished. Length is not important. Write as much as feels right to you for the occasion.

Day 5: Put on your shoes or sandals. Walk or drive to the closest mailbox. Open the mailbox door and insert your letter. Feel the rush of excitement as you imagine it beginning its long journey to your friend or loved one.

Once you have established a new routine/ritual around letter writing, you should find that the task becomes more enjoyable and perhaps, happily habit-forming. Once when I was taking drawing classes and a calligraphy class, for example, I found that overcoming inertia was the hardest part of all. However, once I sat down and focused on the work, suddenly, the time would slip away. Sometimes I even resented having to stop! This is a sure sign that you are onto something that resonates with your heart and soul and is easily repeatable.

Once you have started something new in earnest, says Clear, "it is much easier to continue doing it. A new habit should not feel like a challenge. The actions that follow can be challenging, but the first two minutes should be easy. What you want is a 'gateway habit' that naturally leads you down a more productive path."[213]

Distractions are everywhere, and we need to develop new ways to discipline and finally alter the patterns of behavior that keep us from living our best lives. As Clear points out, simply showing up repeatedly to accomplish a small task is a huge first step. Small changes add up over time, each one a fundamental unit of an overall system of change that allows us to transform our lives. If you stick with those small changes, you will hit a tipping point—the place where it feels easier to maintain your new habits over time.[214]

When you receive your first letter in return, your heart will rejoice, and you will be resolute in your promise to keep your newly formed habit alive, far into the future. You might even wonder why letter writing seemed so difficult to initiate in the first place.

And then, who knows what you might try next? The sky is the limit, and a simple handwritten note was the impetus for all of it.

Tips for Preserving Old Letters

I no longer judge pack rats. I'm speaking about the human kind of pack rat—the people who struggle to let go of personal belongings and memorabilia. If not for their inclination to save things, important artifacts and remnants of our family histories would likely have ended up in landfills, been given away, or recycled long ago.

I came to this realization as we faced the monumental job of emptying out my in-laws' home of forty years. They were what you might describe as "organized pack rats." Like so many of their generation, they kept everything they had ever owned just in case it might be useful sometime in the future. It was their response to having been poor, Depression-age children.

Amid the mountains of belongings, newspapers, magazines, old greeting cards, and clipped recipes, we found many interesting items, including one of the most priceless treasures of all. There, shoved carelessly in the corner of an antique cabinet, were a small number of fragile, tattered, yellowed letters.

After carefully unfolding them, my husband could still read the faded, sepia-colored lettering inside. These letters were written by his great-grandmother Laura, in the prime of her life, some 130 years earlier. The only thing he knew about her was that she had died of typhoid pneumonia at the age of twenty-five, leaving a husband, baby, and family behind to grieve for her.

Dec 8th 1892

Dear Ones All at Home,

Altho' it is now past nine O'clock P.M. I will not feel satisfied if I do not write a few lines. We have been very busy— Between us we have nursed the Baby, washed dishes, swept the dining room & kitchen, dusted & chopped kindling wood— Now Walter is trying to put our sweet Baby girl to sleep— Your loving letter rec'd yesterday A.M. while bathing the Baby. so glad to know all are pretty well. Poor little Mattie I hope her toothache is all gone— I think. Mamma darling you must all look very fine indeed from your description, yes indeed my hat looks very nice, quite stylish. Yes papa I remember Mr Wharton, not by name, but by your description I can quite recall how he looked & spoke— I am very sorry. they have no children have they Seeing that Walter has told you all the church news I have nothing particular to write about for I have only been out to make two calls last Monday since writing last week. A Mrs Hounson & Mrs Mullen (Annie Ball)— Emily will remember her. She inquired

A 130-year-old letter needed careful preservation so that it can be enjoyed by future generations.

For the last thirty years, Laura's sweet portrait had hung on a wall of our home, leaving us to wonder who she was and what she cared about. The letters my husband found, however, helped us to paint a much larger picture of her character. Her letters were warm, expressive, funny, and relatable all these years later. After reading them, we were sad for never having known her.

Now in our hands, we knew it would be up to us to ensure that these treasures were preserved for future generations to enjoy. We began to research the proper ways to archive old paper ephemera, especially letters. I quickly obtained some archival materials, and we have since taken steps to transcribe the letters and to preserve the paper copies for posterity. In doing so, we've honored Laura's life and ensured that her delightful words are not lost to history.

Museums and historical societies do a remarkable job of collecting and cataloging historical letters. However, with such a monumental amount of material to preserve, a good deal of the responsibility for preserving old letters and other family artifacts must fall upon the shoulders of people like you and me who have inherited them. Whether we wanted this responsibility or not, it is now our job to ensure that these historical documents are properly cared for and passed along to the next generation or to historical societies and archives whenever possible.

Preserving historical letters written by famous people or public figures is certainly a worthy pursuit; however, saving and protecting old letters written by "average" citizens is also vitally important. Letters capture the trials and tribulations of our daily lives, our challenges and struggles, our triumphs and failures. They tell us so much about the times in which our predecessors lived, from what they paid for a loaf of bread to their losses and traumas from times of war. Surely, we do not want to lose that history if we can help it.

Unfortunately, when matriarchs and patriarchs of a family die, their belongings can become scattered among family members or, in some cases, end up in a dumpster or in a recycling bin by the curb. If someone takes an interest and decides to save the old family letters, they may hold on to them for a generation. With each subsequent generation, the risk of these documents being lost or destroyed increases.

I confess that in my extended family, we do not yet have a chain-of-custody agreement to ensure that scattered family heirlooms and letters get passed along in a sensible way to the next generations. Without a plan, there is no telling what may happen to family heirlooms as people pass on. Not only do we stand a good chance of losing key pieces of our family's history, but it makes it more difficult for future genealogists and historians to do their research and answer questions for those in the future who may have a stronger curiosity about history.

Retirement Years Can Help

Our retirement years can provide the free time we often dreamed about when we were younger. We finally have the space and time to tackle large projects, such as sorting through and preserving family history, archiving family photos, letters, and other artifacts for the next generation.

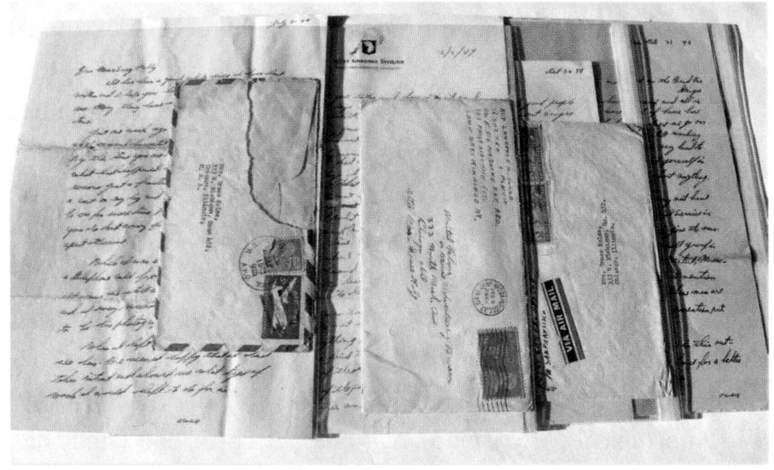

My father's old letters, now properly preserved
and an important part of his legacy.

Archivist and professional genealogist Melissa Barker, in her useful article "Preserving Old Family Letters," outlines the steps we can take to preserve family heirloom letters. The steps are relatively simple; however, they do require a bit of preplanning—purchasing special archival clear plastic sleeves and file boxes, for starters—to protect the letters well:[215]

- Handle your letters as little as possible.
- Do not staple, paper clip, or use glue on the letters.
- Do not laminate letters.
- Do not put Post-it Notes on them.
- Do not secure them with rubber bands.

Step 1. Arrange Letters Chronologically

You may want to begin by grouping together all letters from a category, such as letters from World War II, love letters, letters from camp, and the like. Within each of these groups, organize all letters by the date on the postmark. It is helpful to arrange them in this manner, as sometimes information from one letter is continued on in the next.

Step 2. Unfold the Letters

This step is quite important to preserve letters in the best possible condition. To do so, remove the letters from their envelopes and ensure that each is unfolded. The creases made by folding and unfolding letters can cause damage over time. Eventually, the creases in the paper grow weak and cause the letters to tear into pieces. Laying them flat helps to prevent damage.

Step 3. Encapsulate the Letters

Place each unfolded and flattened letter into its own archival clear sleeve, which you can purchase at any online archival supply store.

These can be somewhat expensive if you need many of them; however, you can purchase them in smaller numbers over several years to keep costs manageable. Ensure that the letter and its envelope are placed in the same sleeve so that they do not get lost or mixed up with another letter. Envelopes often include crucial details, such as dates and the identity and address of the writer, so it is important to keep letters and envelopes together.

Step 4. File and Store Old Letters

Once your letters are chronologically ordered, opened, flattened, and protected, you will now want to file them and store them in one place. As you file them, include biographical details about the person who wrote or received the letters, and any other relevant information.

Place your encapsulated letters into archival file folders and then into archival boxes, being sure to keep the chronological order intact.

Digitizing old letters offers even greater protections. Old letters are very fragile items. They are susceptible to water damage, insects, fires, tornadoes. Sometimes, the ink can fade or the paper can deteriorate and tear. Digitizing letters preserves them for the ages and allows you to share them with family members. By sharing digital copies, you now have them saved in multiple locations, further reducing the risk that they could forever be lost through calamity or neglect.

If not you, who?

Simply No Substitute

On a recent dreary afternoon, I found myself reorganizing an overflowing bookshelf in my basement. Among the stacks of books, I rediscovered my grandmother Margaret's well-worn book of etiquette. Grandma Margaret died when I was three, so I have only a few misty memories of her and not much else except for this book.

My maternal grandmother was raised by a strict aunt and uncle in Scotland and America during Victorian times. Even though her family members had little formal education or wealth, they believed in knowing the basic rules of society, like having manners and following proper protocol on all occasions. In their times, societal rules existed to make communities cooperate more seamlessly and gracefully. It brought a sense of gentility to everyday interactions and personal relationships and made for a more pleasant, civilized, and orderly life for all.

My grandmother's book, *Today's Etiquette*, gives all sorts of advice for living graciously, including rules for how to introduce people to one another, how to set a beautiful table, eat properly, correctly plan a wedding or funeral, and very importantly, how to write social correspondence. In fact, one chapter is devoted entirely to the topic of the handwritten letter.

Reading her book in the present, I marvel—and have a good chuckle—at how far we have fallen from the bar that the author, Lillian Eichler, set in this 1940 rulebook. However, as I read through the chapter on handwritten letters, I came across several interesting and wholly pertinent paragraphs. For one, Eichler heartily encouraged people to continue to write letters:

> You may not be able to write literary letters suitable for publication, letters in the manner of Chesterfield or a Pope. But there is no reason why you cannot write letters that are faultlessly correct, and that give pleasure through their charm of content and their expression of personality.
>
> Those who lament the "the lost art of letter writing" do not realize that the art has not been "lost"—it has simply changed its form. There is a need for mastery in letter-writing more than ever before.[216]

This specific passage of her book reads as if she wrote it today, yet, remarkably, she wrote it more than eighty years ago. In 1940, the telephone was in widespread use as the newest form of communication for middle-class families. The telephone, no doubt, contributed to a significant decline in letter writing, just as the computer has today. Even then, people saw the loss of the handwritten letter as a thing to grieve.

How remarkable that eighty years after Eichler wrote these words, people are still lamenting the loss of handwritten letters. Like Eichler, I also refuse to give in to the notion that the letter is something quaint and past its useful life. Yes, it is old-fashioned (it is more than 2,500 years old, after all). Yes, the letter can be slow and somewhat cumbersome, but Eichler turned out to be right in her time, and I can only hope the future will find me similarly correct. Wouldn't it be wonderful if, in 2100, someone writes yet another book that seeks to keep this amazing art form alive? I can only hope.

As my friend's father wrote in a letter to her in the 1950s: "Correspondence involves answering and asking questions. It involves the interaction of two minds on paper. Some wonderful things (thoughts) can be developed this way but not through the exchange of 'newsletters.' Typical social-personal letters are a mix of both; but there is an obligation and courtesy involved in answering some questions asked by another."

Reimagining Letters for the Twenty-First Century

Eichler was onto something when she suggested that rather than shunt the letter aside completely, we simply change its form. Business letters are still written every day, enabling capitalism and commerce around the world, yet their form has not changed significantly for decades. However, the personal, handwritten letter is almost nonexistent, becoming an endangered form of communication. It may be time to simply reimagine its use for the twenty-first century.

The truth is texts and emails *are* faster than letters and they do address our human need for instant gratification. However, they may not be the only or best choice for every situation. When matters of the heart are involved (and I leave this term undefined because it means something different to everyone), grab for the pen and paper whenever possible. Let us opt for a real letter that can touch our hands, hearts, and minds.

Today, modern society has left millions of people in deep emotional or physical pain or profoundly lonely. Clearly, many people need reminding that they are worthy and loved; men and women who long to see "I love you" written by their lover. We have people ready to take their own lives who need to know they matter to someone. We know people who just want to be heard, affirmed, cherished, and given our undivided attention. They need our letters. They deserve to read "I love you," "You matter to me."

On the flip side, there is also a world of love ready to be freely given. Let's find a way to connect the dots more often with handwritten correspondence. We cannot change the world easily, but we *can* pick up the pen and write, in our own hand, words from our heart—even if they are not perfect. We can add a bit of joy, humor, passion, love,

satire, and delight to the world using a handwritten letter. The beauty of your personality will surely touch someone's heart and perhaps be just the medicine they needed that very day. No other gift given could ever have more value per ounce than the handwritten letter.

A good friend shared a story with me recently as she remembered an especially unhappy time in her life. The saving grace came in the form of a letter. At the time, my friend lived in a dorm at Valparaiso University. She befriended a woman named Kim, who also lived in her building. They hit it off quickly and easily, becoming good friends and confidantes. One thing that my friend appreciated most about Kim was that she was an amazing thinker, listener, and conversationalist; she was someone whom you could talk intelligently and openly with about a wide variety of topics and ideas.

One day, when my friend was feeling especially depressed, she returned to her dorm room to find a letter from Kim taped to her door. Kim's letter expressed how saddened she was to learn that my friend was hurting so badly and how she wished she could do more to help. Kim's kind offering of support affirmed that my friend was heard, understood, and believed, and that she was worthy of love and understanding. Embedded in every line of Kim's letter was evidence of profound respect and caring.

It is not surprising that this letter meant a great deal to my friend, as it arrived at a time when her confidence and sense of self-worth was at an especially low point. This letter served as proof that, for the first time in her life, she had a friend who was authentically concerned for her well-being.

Though the letter is now faded, tattered, and stained, it is kept with loving care in a safe place in my friend's home. Fifty years ago, this letter would play an important role in the process of her emotional healing. Since then, that healing energy has rippled out through my friend to impact the lives of hundreds of other people.

Some Things Never Change (Nor Should They)

We do not want to let go of technology, but at the same time, we don't want to throw away what is most precious and essential to our hearts. We still need letters to be part of our lives. Lillian Eichler described well why they are so important—then and now:

> Your letter goes to a hospital and cheers a friend who is ill. Your letter goes to a disappointed hostess and makes your apologies to her. Your letter goes to an acquaintance, who has been neglected . . . your letter represents you whenever circumstances make it impossible for you to be present personally. And that is why your letter must not only be correct: it must be cordial. It must not only be in good form: it must be gracious, and warm with a touch of your personality.[217]

An eloquent respondent from my letters survey summarized the letter-writing experience so beautifully.

> I have sent and received an ocean of letters in sixty-three years. Before a move some years ago, I sat on the floor in a sea of stamped and hand-addressed envelopes, pulling thin sheets of script, drawings, articles, and cards from them, one by one, reveling in streams of story that had passed between my family and others over many years. Each brought vividly to mind a beloved face, a moment, places, and deep connection to what matters. I am somewhat of a minimalist, so I forced myself to recycle many. But in the end, I put most into bins and moved them to my new home. A friend pointed to them, and I told her, "Someday, when I can do little else, I will sit in a sea of paper again, read them all, seeing signs of my dear ones' development, baby to adult, seeing how we grew, and then, feel gratitude. They represent what has mattered most to me."

With this book, I hope to encourage you to write that occasional letter for that special person or event, or for no reason at all. I believe your efforts matter today more than ever. "These are the micro-moments where we can return to our hearts and cling to them," as Casper ter Kuile states it.[218]

Dozens of reasons exist to take up pen and paper once again. If you do, you just might find it to be one of the most joyful and deeply important activities you have undertaken in many a year.

Final Words

Tender, loving words.

We all need tender, loving words, especially given the difficulties and traumas brought on by COVID-19 and recent civil unrest in this country. If we are lucky, loving words come to us on a regular basis from our nearest and dearest family and friends. Caring, supportive words give us the strength to move through the complex and sometimes gut-wrenching experiences we all grapple with. If we feel loved, we can face daunting challenges and, in most cases, come through them with greater ease and clarity. Indeed, loving words have always brought me great joy as well as soothing comfort.

Over my lifetime, it has been the written word that has proven most valuable to me. Communications delivered through conversation, by telephone, or internet platforms, while meaningful and affirming, are easy to forget or altered by faulty memories. Letters, on the other hand, provide clear documentation of what was, and for that reason, they are more valuable with time.

One such letter immediately comes to mind. I have already told the story of losing my only brother, Lee, who died at age forty-four from cancer. Lee was one of my favorite people in the world. After I moved away from home, I greatly missed his offbeat and hilarious sense of humor and his utterly unique way of telling stories and interpreting life. But there was so much more to my brother. He also had a caring, empathetic heart. Letters allowed him to express himself in a way he could not always reveal in person.

In the summer of my brother's forty-fourth year, when he was diagnosed with Stage 4 malignant brain cancer, he had just settled into a charming bungalow in Alabama and was far from family and friends. Immediately after his terrifying diagnosis, my parents, my sisters, and I created a plan for how we would care for him. My family agreed to rotate caregiving at his home that summer, allowing us time to be with him and to figure out next steps.

When it was my turn to care for Lee, I left my young children in my husband Allen's care, boarded a plane, then rented a car to get to his home in Huntsville. Just before I arrived, Lee had gone through a long, complicated surgery to remove the tumors invading his brain—a dangerous and risky procedure. The doctors had explained that they could only temporarily relieve his symptoms and that the tumors would quickly regrow. They told us that there was no telling how the cancer would begin to affect his body and personality. He could, they said, become physically and mentally impaired, or worst yet, the tumors might make him uncharacteristically angry or even violent. Thankfully, his witty and loving personality never wavered until the last—a real gift to all of us.

Lee had survived the surgery well and was on the mend when I arrived on the scene. As I parked the car on the street in front of his house, I immediately noticed him sitting on his porch swing. He looked amazingly serene, given what he had just been through. His head was partially bandaged, and he wore a bill cap to cover the bald area and the large scar that was still healing.

As I stepped onto the porch, he immediately got up and hugged me for a long time, as if he might never see me again.

"Thank you so much for coming, Lynne," he said. "It's so good to see you, but I feel so bad that you had to leave the kids for so long. Are they going to be okay?"

"Sure," I said. "Allen will take good care of them. I'm not worried at all."

He smiled, and we sat back on his porch swing, feeling the oppressive heat and humidity, and listened to the cicadas. We talked with the same ease we always had. Every word he spoke seemed to have a great weight and importance to it, because I knew there would not be many more conversations like this before things would begin to go terribly wrong.

So, I tried to drink in that moment, but the truth is, I have since forgotten much of our conversation that day. As hard as I tried to remember it all, I was too overwhelmed with sadness to do that. In fact, there was a good deal that happened that week at his home that I cannot recall. It was all a painful and shattering blur. I tried hard to hide the sense of panic and grief I felt as we attended to doctor visits and dealt with the red tape that sadly overshadows a serious illness.

Not long after I returned home from that heart-wrenching week in Alabama, I received a note from Lee. It was short—his boisterous and optimistic cursive writing belied the tragedy of his circumstances. He wrote to me of his gratitude for what I had done to help him, that he would survive the horrible disease he was still battling, and that he had high hopes of seeing my kids again soon.

Tragically, he would die just three months later, leaving a son, parents, four sisters, and many good friends deep in grief.

The solace comes now in still having his letters here in front of me when he no longer can be. Each and every word—funny, often irreverent, and always kind—are treasures I hold dear. Without his letters, I would undoubtedly struggle to remember his words as the years passed. However, reading his letters now brings his great personality back to me in vivid color, if only for a moment. If I close my eyes, I can see him in my memories: there, out in front of me, smiling joyfully as we pedaled to town to spend our allowances, and much later, in my living room, wearing a wide, wistful smile as he held my son for the first time. "You're so lucky!" he said.

Letters help us to weave the tapestry of love that is our lives.

They record our humanity, the better parts of us. And if we write them now, we will still be here on paper a hundred years from now, proving to future generations that the human heart changes little through space and time. Love never dies. Letters ensure that our words and our humanity do not either.

Epilogue

As I write this, COVID-19 is still wreaking havoc and causing long-term illnesses and deaths around the world. I think about the families and the grieving and the feelings of helplessness many of us have had. While all this is true, I must also acknowledge and celebrate the actions of heroic public servants, medical professionals, essential workers, teachers, and researchers, many of whom put themselves and family members at risk to keep the broader population safe.

Like many people, I considered different things I could do to help during the early days of the pandemic. The first thing that came to mind was all the people who would have to be home alone during this time, feeling isolated. My mind immediately turned to what I felt I was good at: writing letters.

One day, while sitting outside, I set a goal for myself: to handwrite a letter to each person I knew who was living alone. I would write at least one letter a day if I could. That list of friends and relatives, for the most part, was quite long. I started with my nephew who lives in Amsterdam in a small apartment, far from his family in the Midwest. Then, it was on to a friend, my ninety-four-year-old aunt, a cousin, another friend, and a niece in Seattle. It was my way of coping with an unknown, of trying to create normalcy during chaos.

Similarly, a member of my friend's writers' group made her own contribution to creating order and remaining steadfast in the middle of the worldwide pandemic. She explains, "I am spending parts of every day in what I think of as a 'ministry of correspondence.' I am writing lots of letters, notes, emails to people I know or sort of know or just know of who are suffering in some way. I think of this as my spiritual practice during the pandemic."

Letters, old or new, provide nuggets of hope we can cling to during these unsettling times. Small gestures like this seem so right. We hope that our letters feel like a warm, long-distance hug to our friends and loved ones. We want them to know that they are not alone, that they are much loved and valued, that they will not be forgotten.

My nephew in Amsterdam was not someone I communicated with much, except at our usual annual holiday parties. I never really expected a response to my pandemic letters, so I took no offense when none arrived. Then one day in 2021, I received an email from him for the first time ever. In it were his simple words of thanks, along with the promise of a gift that would be arriving shortly. One day, his package arrived. Inside was a lovely new fountain pen and some sleek-looking bottles of ink. His unexpected, sweet gift deeply touched my heart. Simple gestures we make do matter, sometimes more than we imagine. If we take the risk to reach out, we might just be surprised by the response.

This terrible virus is a good reminder of how fleeting and unpredictable life can be. Letter writing offers one mechanism for conveying the feelings we hold deep in our hearts but may never be able to say to someone we love face-to-face. Few times in recent history have offered us such lessons in the need to communicate our love.

As a result of the pandemic experience, I vow to move forward and find joy in writing a similar message over and over:

I love you. Thank you for everything.

You are irreplaceable, an important part of my life.

You mean the world to me.

With much love and gratitude,

Lynne

A Letter in Return

I am already excited.
It is a letter from you—
an answer, some news
declaration
revelation made
in your own given hand and maybe
probably
overly punctuated as
I have come to expect, indeed,
as I hope for because
it is you and it is for
only me
"Dear one" it begins
"Hey there" it may court or
coax or soothe as it
answers
like a lob from a friendly
match player ensuring the connection
continues and flows
a crested wave back into the sea
But it is a drink from unsalted waters
not bitter as good messages
treat

no need for a bottle or mystery when
replies carefully cast
deeply pool to sate my delight

My thanks are a given
as I begin my letter in return.

—Julie Kolze Sorensen

Dear Readers,

Please write! I would love to hear from you and about your own letter writing stories and experiences! You can reach me at the following address:

Lynne Kolze
c/o Kolze Creations
PO Box 14313
Saint Paul, MN 55114

I will do my best to respond to as many letters as I can; however, depending on the volume of mail I receive, this may not always be possible. Please know that I will make every effort to read all the letters that reach me.

With gratitude and appreciation,

Lynne

Acknowledgments

First, I must thank the letter writers in my life. I am deeply grateful for the friends, lovers, and family members whose soulful, humorous, and loving words inspired my passion for handwritten letters from an early age. Thank you for sharing yourselves with me in such delightful and endearing ways. You are always close to my heart.

This book would never have been written if not for the gentle nudging of my good friend Judy Helgen. Her love of writing inspired me to try it as a form of creative expression. Our biweekly meetings in her comfortable home, and the wonderful sharing we did there, provided the support and encouragement I needed to see this project through from beginning to end as a first-time author.

My sister, Julie Kolze Sorensen, encouraged me to put pen to paper and to keep it there, just as she learned to do herself when writing her fine poetry. Julie's willingness to read through early drafts of this book, and offer constructive criticism, helped to bring it to fruition. More than anything, I am grateful that she helped me to keep my vision alive, even when I was ready to give it up completely. Julie—you have always been there for me: creative advisor, friend, and mentor. What would I do without you?

Special thanks must go to my patient and supportive friends and family members, some of whom willingly volunteered to read the book in its early stages—then encouraged me anyway! Thoughtful comments and/or loving support were offered by Sandy and Ray Bissonnette, Janna Caywood, Jaentra Green Gardener, Cindy Hilmoe, Nancy Kolze, Janet Kolze, June Matayoshi, Carrie McCabe, Marcia Parker, Shelley Schmidt, Martha Swanson, Lori Nelson, and Todd Timmcke. You have all added great depth and meaning to my life. I thank you from the bottom of my heart.

To the writing professionals that made this book possible, Mary Caroll Moore, Heather McPherson, Julie Sturgeon, and Sara Ensey—each made brilliant contributions and found clever ways to shorten and focus my writing. I am full of appreciation for your talents and insights. And to the folks at Beaver's Pond Press, especially Alicia Ester, I owe my gratitude for guiding me seamlessly through the publishing process. Thanks also to Dan Pitts for his creative design work that brought life to these pages.

To my husband, Allen—your beautiful, witty love letters told me everything I needed to know about you many years ago. What an adventure we have had ever since. To my children, Laura and Ian—becoming your mother was the best thing that ever happened to me. I thank you for your love and support. And always remember my dear ones, love *can* fit into an envelope!

Image Credits

All photographs in this book are owned by the author, with the following exceptions:

Letters Are a Learning Laboratory

Page 32: Courtesy of the Smithsonian National Museum of American History Digital Library, https://www.si.edu/newsdesk/snapshot/thomas-jeffersons-desk.

Letters from Our Grandmothers

Page 95: Courtesy of the New York Library Digital Library, https://digitalcollections.nypl.org/items/d8e81860-f656-0136-3b00-2beeb53765c0.

Artful Flourishes We Don't Forget

Page 169: Courtesy of Lindsey Bugbee of thepostmanknocks.com.
Page 171: Courtesy of the New York Digital Library, https://digitalcollections.nypl.org/items/ce2758c0-cc91-0139-2d9a-0242ac110002.

Mail Art

Page 190: Courtesy of Lindsey Bugbee of thepostmanknocks.com.

Epistolary Art

Page 196: *The Letter* by Mary Cassatt, 1890-91. Courtesy of The Art Institute of Chicago Digital Library, https://www.artic.edu/artworks/13508/the-letter.

A Short History of the Letter

Page 205: Benoît-Louis Prévost's Art of Writing, from Encyclopédie. 1760. Courtesy of The Art Institute of Chicago Digital Library, https://www.artic.edu/artworks/148207/art-of-writing-from-encyclopedie.
Page 206: "George Blake's Letter," by Winslow Homer, 1870. Courtesy of The Smithsonian American Art Museum Digital Library, https://www.si.edu/object/george-blakes-letter-galaxy-january-1870:saam_1996.63.187.

A Letter to the Bridegroom's Oak

Page 225: Armin von Werner/ CC-BY-2.5, WikiMedia. No changes have been made to the original photo.

Sending Letters to a Neighborhood Elf

Page 228: Courtesy of Jim Marvey.

W. Reginald Bray: The Human Letter

Page 243: Courtesy of Zoe James.
Page 245: Courtesy of John Tingey.

Letters Lost and Found

Page 248: Courtesy of Antonios Ntoumas, Pixaby.

Encouraging the Next Generation of Letter Writers

Page 261: Courtesy of Janna Caywood.

Endnotes

Introduction

1 Brandon Gaille, "30 Greeting Card Industry Statistics and Trends," Brandon Gaille Small Business and Marketing Advice, September 6, 2018, retrieved October 28, 2020, https://brandongaille.com/30-greeting-card-industry-statistics-and-trends/.

2 Olivia Hosken, "A Side Effect of the Pandemic? Stationery Sales Are Booming Right Now," *Town and Country*, June 27, 2020.

Why We Still Need Letters

3 Stacy Colino, "How Loneliness Affects Health," *Brain and Life*, October/November 2020.

4 Robert Waldinger, TED Talk, March 15, 2021, retrieved April 10, 2021.

5 Ibid.

A Treasured Memento

6 Alli Hoff Kosik, "Why Handwriting Letters Still Matter in a Digital World," Brit + Co., May 1, 2018, https://www.brit.co/value-of-handwritten-letters/.

7 "Millennials Are Keeping Handwriting Alive," *New York Post*, April 12, 2018.

Skip the Gym: Why Letter Writing Is Good for Us

8 "More Children Are Becoming Near-Sighted. These New Glasses Might Help," Healthline, updated May 7, 2018, https://www.healthline.com/health-news/more-children-becoming-nearsighted-these-new-glasses-might-help.

9 "Study: Want to Be Happier? Be More Grateful," Science Daily, December 27, 2008, https://www.sciencedaily.com/releases/2008/11/081125113005.htm.

10 Ibid.

11 Ibid.

The Joy of Anticipation

12 "The Joy of Anticipation," Psychologies, April 8, 2014, https://www.psychologies.co.uk/the-joy-of-anticipation/.

Letters Are a Learning Laboratory

13 Dennis Depcik, letter to the author, January 2022.

Letter Writing as Spiritual Practice

14 Rachel Naomi Remen, *Kitchen Table Wisdom: Stories That Heal* (New York: Riverhead Books, 2006), p. 284.

15 Casper ter Kuile, *The Power of Ritual: Turning Everyday Activities into Soulful Practices* (New York: HarperOne, 2020), p. 26.

Letters Can Save Lives

16 "Caring Letters Prevent Suicide," Stanford University, citing J. A. Motto and A. G. Bostrom, "A Randomized Controlled Trial of Postcrisis Suicide Prevention," *Psychiatric Services* 52, no. 6 (2001): 828–833.

17 Ibid.

18 Ibid.

19 "Current Funded Research," Military Suicide Research Consortium, retrieved February 21, 2022, https://msrc.fsu.edu/funded-research/bt-msg.

Letters Encourage Our Development

20 Permission for use granted courtesy of the Fred Rogers Company, 2021.

Thank-You Letters: Why Showing Appreciation Never Goes Out of Style

21 Richard Gunderman, "Why Gratitude Is So Good for You (and for Those Around You)," Intellectual Takeout, August 1, 2018, https://intellectualtakeout.org/2018/08/why-gratitude-is-so-good-for-you-and-for-those-around-you/.

22 Thanksgiving.com, "4 Reasons Gratitude is Good for You," *USA Today*, November 17, 2017.

Gratitude Letters: Beyond the Simple Thank-You

23 Thanksgiving.com, "4 Reasons Gratitude is Good for You," *USA Today*, November 17, 2017.

24 Neel Burton, "Why Gratitude Is So Hard," *Psychology Today*, December 24, 2016.

25 Summer Allen, "Why Is Gratitude So Hard for Some People?," *Greater Good Magazine*, May 10, 2018.

26 Burton, "Why Gratitude Is So Hard."

Be Still My Heart: Long Live the Love Letter

27 Dennis Depcik, *Wouldn't It Be Something?* (West Conshohocken, PA: Infinity Publishing, 2013), p. 2.

28 Ibid., p. 222.

29 "About the Correspondence between John and Abigail Adams," Massachusetts Historical Society, retrieved February 23, 2020, https://www.masshist.org/digitaladams/archive/letter/.

30 Stephen Adams, "Valentine's Day: Technology Is Killing Romance," *Telegraph*, February 9, 2009.

A Soldier's Letters Home

31 *The War*, WETA Public Television, Washington and American Lives II Film Project, September 2007._

32 Dennis Depcik, *Wouldn't It Be Something?* (West Conshohocken, PA: Infinity Publishing, 2013), p.15.

Letters from a Stranger

33 "Feeling Lonely? So Are a Lot of Other People, Survey Finds," CBS News, October 12, 2016, https://www.cbsnews.com/news/many-americans-are-lonely-survey-finds/.

34 Ibid.

35 "A 98-Year-Old Woman Sends 7k Letters to Troops," ABC 13, retrieved February 23, 2022, https://abc13.com/society/a-98-year-old-woman-sends-7k-letters-to-troops/2047396.

36 Diana Chao, "Why I Handwrite Letters to Strangers," National Alliance on Mental Illness, August 27, 2018, https://www.nami.org/Blogs/NAMI-Blog/August-2018-/Why-I-Handwrite-Letters-to-Strangers.

37 Martha Ann Overland, "'Dear Stranger': Connecting People One Letter at a Time," National Public Radio, April 11, 2020, https://www.npr.org/2020/04/11/830419144/dear-stranger-connecting-people-one-letter-at-a-time.

38 The World Needs More Love Letters, retrieved December 1, 2019, http://www.moreloveletters.com.

39 Overland, "'Dear Stranger.'"

40 Ibid.

41 Julie Kendrick, "After Losing Her Mom to Leukemia, Minnesota Woman Delivers Cards to Ill Kids," *Star Tribune*, April 1, 2022.

The Sympathy Letter

42 Steven Petrow, "Joe Biden's Wise Words About Death Helped Me Understand the Realities of Life," *Washington Post*, April 15, 2021.

Letters That Hurt

43 Anna Holmes, ed., *Hell Hath No Fury: Women's Letters from the End of the Affair* (New York: Ballentine, 2004), p. 107.

44 Anthony Trollope, *Can You Forgive Her?* (New York: Penguin Classics, 1974).

45 Holmes, *Hell Hath No Fury*, p. 107.

Letters That Heal

46 Karen Baikie and Kay Wilhelm, "Emotional and Physical Health Benefits of Expressive Writing," *Advances in Psychiatric Treatment* 11 (2005): 338–346.

47 Ibid.

48 John F. Evans, "Transactional Writing: Letters That Heal," *Psychology Today*, March 24, 2014.

49 Ibid.

50 Ibid.

51 Ibid.

52 Bhavna Raithatha, "Writing as Therapy," Counselling Director, March 16, 2021, https://www.counselling-directory.org.uk/memberarticles/writing-as-therapy.

53 Evans, "Transactional Writing."

54 Ibid.

55 Shaka Senghor, "Why Your Worst Deeds Don't Define You," TED, June 23, 2014.

56 Lolly Bowean, "'I'll Never Leave Your Side': His Father's Letters Helped Him Endure 10 Years in Prison," *Guardian*, January 3, 2022, https://www.theguardian.com/world/2022/jan/03/shaka-senghor-letters-sons.

57 Ibid.

Pen Pal Letters: A Whole New World Awaits

58 Jasmine June Cabanaw, "5 Facts You Didn't Know About Letter Writing," Albert Flynn DeSilver, October 7, 2015, https://albertflynndesilver.com/5-facts-you-didnt-know-about-letter-writing/.

The Round Robin: The Letter That Keeps on Giving

59 Michael Hogan, "What Round Robin Letters Say . . . and What They Really Mean," *Telegraph*, December 18, 2016.

60 Kelly Viancourt, "Round Robin Takes Flight," *Oberlin Alumni Magazine*, summer 2001.

61 Asha Anchan, "Family Uses Round-Robin System for Writing Letters," *Norfolk Daily News*, June 11, 2011.

62 Ibid.

The Legacy Letter

63 Constance Gustke, "The Ethical Will, an Ancient Concept, Is Revamped for the Tech Age," *New York Times*, November 1, 2014.

64 "Ethical Wills and Legacy Letters Are Different Than a Memoirs, an Autobiographies, Oral Histories or Legal Wills," Legacy Letters, retrieved February 22, 2020, https://www.legacyletter.org/legacy-letters/ethical-wills/.

65 Constance Gustke, "The Ethical Will, an Ancient Concept, Is Revamped for the Tech Age," *New York Times*, November 1, 2014.

66 Rachel Freed, "Write a Legacy Letter Today!," Huffington Post, August 29, 2013, https://www.huffpost.com/entry/writing-letters_b_3831203.

67 Ibid.

68 Deborah Quilter, "The Ethical Will: Life Is About More Than Your Possessions," Market Watch, April 11, 2019, https://www.marketwatch.com/story/why-you-need-to-write-an-ethical-will-2019-04-25.

69 Ibid.

70 Ray Bradbury, *Fahrenheit 451* (New York: Ballantine Books, 1953), p. 156.

71 Libby Cohen, "Vietnam War Author Reveals the Victories of Fatherhood in New Book," *Texas Standard*, October 11, 2019.

Artful Flourishes We Don't Forget

72 Jessica Rixom, Erik Mas, and Brett Rixom, "Presentation Matters: The Effect of Wrapping Neatness on Gift Attitudes," *Journal of Consumer Psychology* 30, no. 2 (2020): 329–338, https://myscp.onlinelibrary.wiley.com/doi/abs/10.1002/jcpy.1140.

73 Robert Z. Pearlman, "Pluto Stamp Aboard NASA's New Horizons Probe Sets Guinness World Record," Space.com, July 19, 2016, https://www.space.com/33478-pluto-stamp-nasa-new-horizons-world-record.html.

74 Ashley Davis, "The History Behind . . . Signet Rings," National Jeweler, September 7, 2016, https://www.nationaljeweler.com/articles/9513-the-history-behind-signet-rings.

75 "The History and Resurgence of Wax Seals" Stamps Direct, August 2, 2013, https://www.stampsdirect.co.uk/blog/the-history-and-resurgence-of-wax-seals.html.

76 *Encyclopedia Britannica Online*, s.v. "Sealing wax," retrieved February 2022, https://www.britannica.com/technology/sealing-wax.

77 Ibid.

78 *Encyclopedia Britannica Online*, s.v. "Embossing," retrieved February 2022, https://www.britannica.com/art/embossing.

Doodles, Drawings, and Other Delights

79 Nolan Feeney, "Here's Why, How and What You Should Doodle to Boost Your Mind and Creativity," *Fast Company*, August 14, 2014.

80 Linda Lear, *Beatrix Potter: A Life in Nature* (New York: St. Martin's Press, 2007), pp. 142–145.

Letters That Think Outside the Envelope

81 "World's Smallest Post Service," Leaf Cutter Designs, https://www.leafcutterdesigns.com/tiny-mail/.

Mail Art

82 Quoted in Grace Glueck, "What Happened? Nothing," *New York Times*, April 11, 1965.

83 "Mail Art," Tate, retrieved February 24, 2022, https://www.tate.org.uk/art/art-terms/m/mail-art.

Epistolary Art

84 "Epistolary," Literary Devices, retrieved on February 13, 2020, https://literarydevices.net/epistolary/.

85 Jesse Doogan, "100 Must-Read Epistolary Novels from the Past and Present," Book Riot, August 24, 2016, https://bookriot.com/100-epistolary-novels-from-the-past-and-present/.

86 Zoe Jackson, "Intergenerational Musical Brings Together Actors, Ages 11–87 in Hopkins," *Star Tribune*, January 17, 2020.

87 Ibid.

88 Ibid.

A Short History of the Letter

89 https://www.handwrittenletters.com, retrieved April 6, 2020 (website discontinued).

90 "Papyrus: A Brief History," Dartmouth Ancient Books Lab, Historical Background Section, May 23, 2016, https://sites.dartmouth.edu/ancientbooks/2016/05/23/67/.

91 Lydia Pyne, "A History of Ink in Six Objects," History Today, May 16, 2018, https://www.historytoday.com/history-matters/history-ink-six-objects.

92 "Timeline of Paper and Papermaking," History of Paper, retrieved February 28, 2020, https:// www.historyofpaper.net/paper-history/timeline-of-paper/.

93 "The History of Pens," Journal Shop, retrieved February 28, 2020, https://www.thejournalshop.com/en-us/blogs/the-journal/the-history-of-pens.

94 "History of Letter Writing," Time Toast, retrieved June 21, 2020, https://www.timetoast.com/timelines/history-of-letter-writing/.

95 Ibid.

96 "History and Facts About Handwritten Letters," Graphs.net, retrieved February 28, 2020, https://graphs.net/history-and-facts-about-handwritten-letters.html.

97 "Ts'ai Lun," Encyclopedia.com, retrieved June 23, 2020, https://www.encyclopedia.com/science/encyclopedias-almanacs-transcripts-and-maps/tsai-lun.

98 "Timeline of Paper and Papermaking," History of Paper.

99 Carlos Tifa, "The Writing Instrument (The Reed and Quill) and Ink," Dartmouth, retrieved February 24, 2022, https://sites.dartmouth.edu/ancientbooks/2016/05/23/the-writing-instrument-the-reed-and-quill-and-ink/.

100 "Timeline of Paper and Papermaking," History of Paper.

101 Ibid.

102 Ibid.

103 Sarah Cantavalle, "The History of Papermaking From Its Origins to the Present Day," Pixartprinting, April 5, 2019, https://www.pixartprinting.co.uk/blog/history-paper/.

104 "History," Barchowsky Fluent Handwriting, retrieved January 25, 2020, https://www.bfhhandwriting.com/history-of-cursive-handwriting.

105 "Italic Calligraphy for Beginners," Lettering Daily, retrieved April 5, 2022, https://www.lettering-daily.com/italic-calligraphy/.

106 Mary Bellis, "History of the United States Postal Service," ThoughtCo., updated August 20, 2016, https://www.thoughtco.com/history-of-the-united-states-postal-service-4076789.

107 "The History of the Pencil: The Earliest Forms of Self-Expression," Pencils.com, March 29, 2022, https://pencils.com/pages/the-history-of-the-pencil.

108 Bellis, "History of the United States Postal Service."

109 "The History of Pens," Journal Shop.

110 Ibid.

111 Bellis, "History of the United States Postal Service."

112 "History and Facts About Handwritten Letters," Graphs.net.

113 Bellis, "History of the United States Postal Service."

114 "Timeline of Paper and Papermaking," History of Paper.

115 "History and Facts About Handwritten Letters," Graphs.net.

116 Ibid.

117 "Pony Express," National Park Service, retrieved February 24, 2022, https://www.nps.gov/poex/learn/historyculture/index.htm.

118 "The History of Pens," Journal Shop.

119 "History and Facts About Handwritten Letters," Graphs.net.

120 Palmer Method, retrieved February 24, 2022, https://thepalmermethod.com/.

121 "National Letter Writing Day—December 7, 2022," National Today, retrieved December 9, 2019, https://nationaltoday.com/national-letter-writing-day/.

122 "The History of Pens," Journal Shop.

123 "When Was the First Computer Invented?," Computer Hope, updated December 30, 2021, retrieved March 2, 2020, https://www.computerhope.com/issues/ch000984.htm.

124 Douglas Crowe, "Why Steve Jobs's Passion for Calligraphy Is an Important Example for You," *Entrepreneur*, August 8, 2021, https://www.entrepreneur.com/article/377943.

125 "The History of Pens," Journal Shop.

126 "Paper Recycling Facts," University of Southern Indiana, retrieved December 1, 2020, https://www.usi.edu/recycle/paper-recycling-facts.

127 Ibid.

128 Ian Dear, *Escape and Evasion: POW Breakouts, and Other Great Escapes in World War II* (Gloucestershire, UK: History Press Ltd., 2010), p. 32.

129 Nancy Werteen, "How Handwriting Stimulates the Brain," WMZ News, retrieved January 19, 2022.

130 "The History of Ink," *Week*, retrieved April 8, 2022, https://www.theweek.co.uk/innovation-at-work/63310/the-history-of-ink.

131 Ibid.

132 Ibid.

133 Ibid.

134 Ibid.

135 Troy Patterson, "Fountain Pen Sales Are Surging, Despite Flat Luxury Global Sales," *Bloomberg*, February 2, 2017, https://www.bloomberg.com/news/articles/2017-02-02/fountain-pen-sales-are-surging-despite-flat-luxury-global-sales#xj4y7vzkg.

136 Charles Huang, "Why Stationery Fans Are Flocking for Japan's Y5 Million Fountain Pens," *Tokyo Weekender*, February 18, 2020, https://www.tokyoweekender.com/2020/02/why-fans-are-flocking-for-japans-%C2%A55-million-fountain-pens/.

137 Ibid.

138 Ibid.

The Postmark/Stamp Cancel

139 Charles Huang, "Why Stationery Fans Are Flocking for Japan's Y5 Million Fountain Pens," *Tokyo Weekender*, February 18, 2020, https://www.tokyoweekender.com/2020/02/why-fans-are-flocking-for-japans-%C2%A55-million-fountain-pens/.

140 "Understanding Stamp Cancels," PostcardValues.com, retrieved February 5, 2020, http://www.postcardvalues.com/cancellations.html.

141 Ibid.

142 Les Winick, "Collecting Postmarks: A Key to Unlocking the World of Philately," *Chicago Tribune*, November 17, 1985.

143 Ibid.

144 Geoff Manaugh and Nicola Twilley, "In the 1500s, Mail Disinfection Was Really,

Really Weird," *Atlantic*, July 20, 2021.

The Postcard: A Simple Feast for the Eyes

145 "Vintage Postcard History," Vintage American, retrieved April 9, 2022, https://www.vintage-american.com/vintage-postcard-history.

146 "A Postcard History," Smithsonian Institution Archives, retrieved February 24, 2022, https://siarchives.si.edu/history/featured-topics/postcard/postcard-history.

147 Ibid.

148 Ibid.

149 Ibid.

150 "Vintage Postcard History," Vintage American.

151 "A Postcard History," Smithsonian Institution Archives.

152 "Collecting Vintage Real Photo Postcards," PostcardValues.com, retrieved April 9, 2022, https://postcardvalues.com/realphotopostcards.html.

153 "Postcard Collecting," University of Maryland Libraries, retrieved April 9, 2022, https://exhibitions.lib.umd.edu/postcards/collecting.

154 Ibid.

155 Jeanette Settembre, "Postcards Are Becoming Extinct and 5 Other Industries Millennials Are Killing," Market Watch, September 30, 2017, https://www.marketwatch.com/story/postcards-are-becoming-extinct-and-5-other-industries-millennials-are-killing-2017-09-30.

A Letter to the Bridegroom's Oak

156 Jeff Maysh, "The Matchmaking Tree and the Lonely Postman," *Atlantic*, June 10, 2019, updated June 15, 2020, https://www.theatlantic.com/health/archive/2019/06/the-postman-at-the-bridegrooms-oak/591892/.

157 Ibid.

158 Ibid.

Sending Letters to a Neighborhood Elf

159 Mr. Little Guy, retrieved September 25, 2020, http://mrlittleguy.com/.

160 John Windrow, "Lake Walkers Leave Notes for Tree Elf, and He Writes Back," *Star Tribune*, July 4, 1995.

161 Paul Levy, "The Original Lake Harriet Elf (In Business Since 1995), A Competing Lake Harriet Elf (Now Open, 30 Yards Away)," *Star Tribune*, July 26, 2003.

162 "Should I Stay, or Should I Go?," *Star Tribune*, July 11, 1999.

163 John Windrow, "Lake Harriet's Elf Tree Survives a Brief Scare," *Star Tribune*, June 16, 1998.

164 Ibid.

165 Boyd Huppert, "Neighborhood Elf Reflects on 25 Years of Answering Notes Left in His Tree," KARE 11 News, November 23, 2020.

The Subtle, Loving Language of . . . a *Postage Stamp*?

166 "The Secret Language of Postage Stamps," Katemade Designs, retrieved February 24, 2020, https://katemadedesigns.blogspot.com/2017/05/the-secret-language-of-postage-stamps.html#.XlQ3irGJLIU.

167 William Cochrane, "The Language of Stamps," Philatelic Database, May 1, 2013, http://www.philatelicdatabase.com/nostalgia/the-language-of-stamps/.

168 Ibid.

169 Ibid.

170 Jake Rossen, "Why Do We Put Stamps on the Upper-Right Corner?," Mental Floss, May 25, 2016, https://www.mentalfloss.com/article/80165/why-do-we-put-stamps-upper-right-corner.

The Bird-Brained Letter Carrier

171 Mary McMahon, "What Is Pigeon Post?" Historical Index, January 30, 2022, https://www.historicalindex.org/what-is-pigeon-post.htm.

172 "How Far Can Pigeons Fly? It's Almost Unbelievable!," Bird Watching USA, retrieved February 24, 2022, https://www.birdwatchingusa.org/how-far-can-pigeons-fly.

173 "How Do Homing Pigeons Find Home?," Wonderopolis, retrieved February 24, 2022, https://wonderopolis.org/wonder/how-do-homing-pigeons-find-home.

174 "The Pigeon in History," Pigeon Control Resource Centre, retrieved April 20, 2021, https://www.pigeoncontrolresourcecentre.org/html/the-pigeon-in-history.html.

175 Ibid.

176 Ibid.

177 Joe Razes, "Pigeons of War," *America in World War II*, August 2007.

178 Mike Dash, "Closing the Pigeon Gap," *Smithsonian*, April 17, 2012.

179 Maneka Sanjay Gandhi, "A Fascinating History of the Carrier Pigeons," *Kashmi Observer*, July 6, 2020.

180 William Grimes, "Rising Above the Image of a Rodent with Wings," *New York Times*, November 15, 2006.

181 "The Pigeon in History," Pigeon Control Resource Centre.

182 Ibid.

W. Reginald Bray: The Human Letter

183 John Tingey, *The Englishman Who Posted Himself and Other Curious Objects* (New York: Princeton Architectural Press, 2010), p. 24.

184 Ibid.

185 Ibid., p. 47.

186 Ibid., pp. 27, 80.

187 Ibid., p. 80.

188 Ibid., pp. 69, 76.

189 Ibid., pp 73–75.

190 Ibid., p. 67.

191 Ibid., p. 34.

192 Ibid., p.156.

193 Ibid., p. 156

194 Ibid., p. 165.

Letters Lost and Found

195 Melissa Breyer, "12 Amazing Message-in-a-Bottle Stories," Treehugger, October 28, 2021, https://www.treehugger.com/message-in-a-bottle-striking-stories-of-letters-sent-to-sea-4864055.

196 "Christopher Columbus' Message in a Bottle Is Still Waiting to Be Discovered Somewhere on Planet Earth," *Appalachian Magazine*, May 27, 2017.

197 Breyer, "12 Amazing Message-in-a-Bottle Stories."

198 Ibid.

199 Ibid.

200 Rachel Swatman, "World's Oldest Message in a Bottle Confirmed—132 Years After Being Overthrown Overboard," Guinness World Records, March 8, 2018, https://www.guinnessworldrecords.com/news/2018/3/worlds-oldest-message-in-a-bottle-confirmed-132-years-after-being-thrown-overb-517329.

201 Ibid.

202 Aislinn Laing, "Is It Better to Love or Be Loved? Message in a Bottle Discovered 15 Months Later and 5000 Miles Away," *Telegraph*, May 15, 2012.

Mailboxes That Spark Delight

203 Jennifer Nalewicki, "Whale Mail Is the New Snail Mail at the World's First Underwater Post Office," *Smithsonian*, August 9, 2017, https://www.smithsonianmag.com/travel/worlds-first-underwater-post-office-180964385/.

204 "Crazy Underwater Mailboxes Around the World," Mailbox Big Box, August 1, 2016, retrieved January 14, 2020, https://mailboxbigbox.com/blogs/blog/crazy-underwater-mailboxes-around-the-world.

205 Michael McCarthy, "Galapagos Offers the World's Strangest Mailbox," *Province*, December 14, 2016, https://theprovince.com/travel/international-travel/galapagos-offers-the-worlds-strangest-mail-box.

206 Brian Ashcraft, "Unique Japanese Mail Boxes Are Wonderful in Rain or Shine," Kotaku, July 31, 2013, https://kotaku.com/unique-japanese-mail-boxes-are-wonderful-in-rain-or-shi-972354712.

207 Kristine Alexander, "10 Craziest Post Offices on Earth (and Beyond)," Top Tenz, May 22, 2017, https://www.toptenz.net/10-craziest-post-offices-earth-beyond.php.

Letter Writing in a Sea of Distractions

208 James Clear, "Why Is It So Hard to Form Good Habits?," James Clear's website, retrieved October 23, 2019, https://jamesclear.com/why-is-it-so-hard-to-form-good-habits.

209 James Clear, "How to Build a Habit: This is Your Strategy Guide," James Clear's website, retrieved April 8, 2022, https://jamesclear.com/habit-guide.

210 James Clear, "Lesson 2: The Two-Minute Rule for Building Lasting Habits," James Clear's website, retrieved February 6, 2022.

211 Clear, "Why Is It So Hard to Form Good Habits?"

212 James Clear, "How to Stop Procrastinating," James Clear's website, retrieved October 25, 2021, https://jamesclear.com/how-to-stop-procrastinating.

213 Ibid.

214 Ibid.

Tips for Preserving Old Letters

215 "Preserving Old Family Letters," Genealogist in the Archives, October 20, 2018, retrieved December 30, 2021, https://agenealogistinthearchives.blogspot.com/2018/10/preserving-old-family-letters.html.

Simply No Substitute

216 Lillian Eichler, *Today's Etiquette* (City, ST: Publisher Name, Year), p. 62, courtesy of the Lillian Eichler Watson Estate.

217 Ibid., pp. 62–63.

218 Casper ter Kuile, *The Power of Ritual: Turning Everyday Activities into Soulful Practices* (New York: Harper One, 2020), p. 184.

About the Author

Lynne Kolze grew up near Chicago but has called the Twin Cities her home for over thirty years. Before she began writing nonfiction, she earned bachelor's degrees in natural resources and water resources management and a master's degree in public affairs from Indiana University. Kolze's guiding passion was public service, beginning her career as an environmental planner for the US Environmental Protection Agency and later working for the Minnesota Pollution Control Agency. She has extensive experience in writing, public speaking, policy making, and citizen engagement.

Kolze enjoys connecting with her friends and family whether in person, by phone, or through letter writing. She finds joy and meaning in the soulful art of handwritten letters, believing this form of communication is often the most authentic, joyful, and remarkable of all. Kolze also enjoys tending her gardens, traveling, hiking with her husband, Allen, and spending time with her adult children, Laura and Ian.